HOW TO FIX THE WELFARE STATE
Some ideas for better social services

Paul Spicker

First published in Great Britain in 2022 by

Policy Press, an imprint of
Bristol University Press
University of Bristol
1-9 Old Park Hill
Bristol
BS2 8BB
UK
t: +44 (0)117 954 5940
e: bup-info@bristol.ac.uk

Details of international sales and distribution partners are available at
policy.bristoluniversitypress.co.uk

© Paul Spicker 2022

British Library Cataloguing in Publication Data
A catalogue record for this book is available from the British Library

ISBN 978-1-4473-6459-7 hardcover
ISBN 978-1-4473-6460-3 paperback
ISBN 978-1-4473-6461-0 ePub
ISBN 978-1-4473-6462-7 ePdf

Cover design: Liam Roberts
Front cover image: David Thomas Simonds and *The Guardian*

Bristol University Press and Policy Press use environmentally responsible
print partners.

Printed and bound in Great Britain by CMP, Poole

Contents

About the author

Paul Spicker is Emeritus Professor of Public Policy at the Robert Gordon University, Aberdeen. His research includes studies of poverty, need and service delivery; he has worked as a consultant for a range of agencies in social welfare provision. His books include:

- *Stigma and social welfare* (Croom Helm, 1984)
- *Principles of social welfare* (Routledge, 1988)
- *Social housing and the social services* (Longmans, 1989)
- *Poverty and social security: concepts and principles* (Routledge, 1993)
- *Planning for the needs of people with dementia* (with D S Gordon, Avebury, 1997)
- *Social protection: a bilingual glossary* (co-editor with J-P Révauger, Mission-Recherche, 1998)
- *Social policy in a changing society* (with Maurice Mullard, Routledge, 1998)
- *The welfare state: a general theory* (Sage, 2000)
- *Liberty, equality and fraternity* (Policy Press, 2006)
- *Policy analysis for practice* (Policy Press, 2006)
- *Poverty: an international glossary* (co-editor with Sonia Alvarez Leguizamon and David Gordon, Zed, 2007)
- *The idea of poverty* (Policy Press, 2007)
- *The origins of modern welfare* (Peter Lang, 2010)
- *How social security works* (Policy Press, 2011)
- *Reclaiming individualism* (Policy Press, 2013)
- *Social policy: theory and practice* (Policy Press, 2014)
- *Arguments for welfare* (Rowman & Littlefield, 2017)
- *What's wrong with social security benefits?* (Policy Press, 2017)
- *Thinking collectively: social policy, collective action and the common good* (Policy Press, 2019)
- *The poverty of nations: a relational perspective* (Policy Press, 2020)

A range of his published work is available on open access at http://spicker.uk

1

The welfare state

There are many reasons why governments provide welfare services. Some are moral. There are principled arguments based on need, common humanity and rights. There are widely held values, such as independence, capacity and dignity, all of which are enhanced when citizens have basic security. We might well consider welfare to be the right thing to do if it is consistent with the teachings of major religions, or principles of humanitarianism, benevolence and altruism. Providing welfare may be treated as fulfilling moral obligations to the people who are being protected, such as older people who have contributed to society. It may be the right thing to do simply because it makes people's lives better.[1]

Some of the arguments for welfare services are about collective action. The provision of welfare is an expression of mutual responsibility, or solidarity; it represents both the moral responsibilities we have to each other, and it reinforces them. It promotes social cohesion and inclusion. Welfare is a tangible expression of citizenship, the status and rights we have as part of a political community.[2] Welfare furthers the common good: the interests that people have in common, the interests they share as members of a community or members of a society, and the things which are needed for the maintenance and reproduction of a society. And cooperation for mutual benefit makes sense, even from the point of view of self-interested individuals. When they can, most people make collective arrangements with others for their mutual benefit, and to further their common and shared interests — that is how insurance works. In many societies, welfare arrangements have begun with voluntary and independent provision, and the state has only become engaged with the activity belatedly.[3]

Then there are economic arguments. The provision of welfare has proved to be a useful tool in the management of the economy. It maintains the workforce; it builds human capital; it is an investment in people for the future. It helps to promote economic development. A casual reader of the British press may well gain the impression that welfare provision is a fetter on the economy. If anything, the opposite is true — richer countries tend, in general, to have better welfare systems. It is difficult to prove a link conclusively, because that might simply be a sign that richer countries can

---

[1] P Spicker, 2017, *Arguments for welfare*, London: Rowman & Littlefield.
[2] T H Marshall, 1982, *The right to welfare*, London: Heinemann.
[3] See P Spicker, 2000, *The welfare state: a general theory*, London: Sage.

afford to have better systems. What is clearly not true is to suppose that the British welfare state is expensive, when compared with systems in other countries. The National Health Service (NHS) consumes rather less, as a proportion of GDP, than systems such as those in France or the USA which rely more heavily on private health care. That is partly because the NHS has been able to hold demand in check; partly because it has been able to use its purchasing power to drive hard bargains; but also because private systems rely on charging, finance mechanisms and duplication of effort to produce competition, functions which the NHS does not need to have.

Many of the world's 'welfare states', despite the name, are not run by government. Systems of health and social security are typically delivered by a combination of state, voluntary and mutualist arrangements.[4] However, government is the provider of last resort, and it has generally been the case, in almost every country, that that role has led to a slow but progressive increase in the extent to which the state is engaged with social protection.[5] Government can fill the holes left by private provision. Filling holes is intrinsically an inefficient process, but the inefficiency – that is, the average cost of a unit of activity – can be diminished by doing things more generally. The USA's ramshackle, patchy and staggeringly expensive health care system offers a salutary warning.[6] If we want services to be delivered to a minimum standard, government can regulate it. If we want the services to be uniform – one of the driving imperatives in the NHS has been the attempt to avoid a 'postcode lottery', offering the same protection everywhere – it is almost impossible to do this within the patchwork services offered by private and voluntary provision. And if the service is intended to exercise some kind of control over people's behaviour – as it has been in (for example) urban planning, or child protection, or social work with criminal justice – it is not impossible to delegate this in part to independent agencies, but there are obvious problems in ensuring that what is done is legitimate and consistent with democratic governance. There is a strong pragmatic argument for mobilising the resources of the state to do whatever needs doing. That, after all, is what government is there for. Government, as the conservative philosopher Edmund Burke argued, is only 'a contrivance of human wisdom to provide for human wants'.[7]

---

[4] See, for example, P Baldwin, 1990, *The politics of social solidarity*, Cambridge: Cambridge University Press.

[5] See ILO, 2017, *World social protection report 2017–19*, Geneva: International Labour Office, Figure 1.1, p 5.

[6] J Knickman, B Elbel, 2018, *Jonas and Kovner's health care delivery in the United States*, New York: Springer.

[7] E Burke, 1790, *Reflections on the revolution in France*, New York: Holt, Rinehart and Winston, 1959 edition, p 71.

All told, the case for the welfare state is overwhelming. There are variations – the principles which are applied to people who are disabled, unemployed or elderly are different, wherever one looks – but virtually every developed country in the world has accepted at least some of those arguments, and in recent years most middle-income countries have been taking steps to join them.[8] Around the world, governments have been making commitments to spending on health, education and cash support.[9] There has been a proliferation of new democracies in the course of the last thirty years: the first thing they promise their citizens is not (as some of the literature supposes[10]) defence and public order, but prosperity. As some of the leading philosophers have put it, *Salus populi suprema lex*: the welfare of the people is the highest law.[11]

The challenge to the welfare state

Despite the strength of the case for welfare, it is also true that for more than sixty years – almost since its inception – the British welfare state has been subjected to sustained, sometimes strident, criticism from people who think it shouldn't exist. The main charges against it are that it is unaffordable, fuelled by high taxation, inferior to market-based solutions, and that it undermines moral fibre. The welfare state, the critics say, makes things worse than they would be if it wasn't there. It 'infantilises' the poor.[12] Its services are depicted as being unsustainable. So, the NHS is said to be 'collapsing ... disastrous ... a monumental failure' and 'on its deathbed'.[13] (This was written some time before the covid crisis, but it was evident rubbish then as now.[14]) We might read: 'The welfare state has gone from a safety net to a production line of damaged personalities.'[15] Another pundit complains: 'Britain must

---

[8] L Leisering (ed), 2021, *One hundred years of social protection*, Cham, Switzerland: Palgrave Macmillan.

[9] M Shafik, 2017, *Beveridge 2.0: Sustainable societies and the welfare state*, London: LSE.

[10] For example, A Smith, 1776, *The wealth of nations*, book 5 ch 1; R Nozick, 1974, *Anarchy, state and utopia*, New York: Basic Books.

[11] For example, Thomas Hobbes, 1640, *The elements of law*, ch 9; J Locke, 1689, *Second treatise of civil government*, ch 13.

[12] H Fearn, 2019, How we broke the welfare state, *The Independent*, 26 March, p 38; S Jacobs, 2020, Time to stop the advance of the Covid State, *Daily Telegraph*, 29 October.

[13] S Pipes, 2018, Why does the left want universal health care? Britain's is on its deathbed, *Fortune*, https://fortune.com/2018/07/10/nhs-70-years-uk-britain-single-payer

[14] For a more balanced view, see M Dayan, D Ward, T Gardiner, E Kelly, 2018, *How good is the NHS?*, London: Health Foundation, Institute for Fiscal Studies, King's Fund and Nuffield Trust.

[15] L Bannerman, 2016, Ban me, but I'll still believe the welfare state breeds failure, *The Times*, 5 March.

end the complacency that has infected our national life and stop the merry-go-round of benefits dependency.'[16] The *Daily Telegraph* tells us: 'A system designed as a safety net for the most vulnerable has swelled into an all-consuming client state which stifles aspirations and dignity.'[17]

'Dependency' is a recurring theme in these criticisms. Richard Titmuss described the social services as a response to 'states of dependency' – conditions such as childhood, old age, sickness and unemployment.[18] Dependency in that sense is a normal part of social life: any of us can expect to have periods and stages when we draw on social services. A critical report from the Centre for Policy Studies defines 'dependency' as receiving more from the state, both in cash and in kind, than is paid in income tax.[19] The report begins by using figures that include pensioner households. Yes, the government in the UK does make provision for older people, in the form of pensions. Some of us, and not only the pensioners, think this is rather a good idea. Then the report narrows the focus to people of working age:

> Non-retired households with children seem to be particularly dependent on the state. In 2012/13, 56% of such households received more in benefits than they paid in taxes compared to 25.6% of non-retired households without children. This must in large part be explained by heavier reliance on education spending and other child related cash benefits.[20]

Put this another way. If people have children, and those children go to a state-funded school, they will benefit from state provision, largely paid for through taxation. If people do not have children, they will not benefit in the same way. That implies that the system is mildly redistributive. The redistribution goes, not from rich to poor as such, but 'horizontally', from people without children to families with them. This can also be seen, as pensions can be seen, as a redistribution between different stages of people's lives. If we ask what the welfare state is actually doing, a large proportion of it seems to be a support for older people, support for children or the public provision of education. This, apparently, is undermining our dignity. (Parenting, in my experience, is liable to puncture any lingering sense one has of personal dignity, but I would not attribute that to the actions of the state.)

---

[16] P Dominiczak, 2015, Welfare cuts will 'return the system to sanity', *Daily Telegraph*, 22 June.

[17] *Daily Telegraph*, 2015, The destructive effect of dependency on the state, 15 February, http://www.telegraph.co.uk/news/politics/conservative/11414430/The-destructive-effect-of-dependency-on-the-state.html

[18] R Titmuss, 1955, The social division of welfare, in *Essays on the welfare state*, London: George Allen and Unwin, 1963 edition, pp 42–3.

[19] A Memon, 2015, *Welfare dependency and the size of the state*, Centre for Policy Studies, February.

[20] Memon, 2015, p 5.

The focus on 'aspirations' and 'dignity' is part of a more general claim: that the welfare state corrupts and undermines our character. This is not a new argument. Critics of welfare provision have been making similar arguments for at least 250 years, and probably longer. This, for example, was written in 1783: 'It has been the experience of every country, that a liberal provision for the poor has been followed by sloth, prodigality, and neglect of their families.'[21] At that time, there was no country that might be said to have made a 'liberal provision' for its poor – and certainly not Britain. In the same vein, a later commentator wrote, in 1835:

> Poverty will leave its impress upon all men, both as regards habits and manners, but it was left for the pauper system of England to show that it might be rendered available to the destruction of their feelings, and strike out of the machine of man the mainspring of his moral movements, namely – a sense of shame.[22]

It was not true then. Is it any more true now? There is no good reason to think so, and some to doubt it. The discourse used in the UK in the era of the welfare state has slowly reverted to the discourse that dominated debates in the nineteenth century: the stigmatisation of poverty, the accusation of idleness and unwillingness to work, and the representation of welfare as a public burden. It is all too easy to find commentary in the press or reports on television, built on the premise that people who receive benefits are dependent, demanding, lazy and have a misplaced sense of entitlement. There is a continuing commitment to welfare in some fields, particularly health care, but much of the political debate is highly individualistic, market-oriented and critical of the poor.

At the time of its foundation, the British welfare state was unusual: there were not many governments in the world which had made a general commitment to welfare. Now, welfare is provided by government to some degree in just about every developed economy, and increasingly in many poorer and emerging economies. The UK no longer stands out from the crowd. Its expenditure is modest; its coverage, by comparison with other developed economies, falls somewhere in the middle. When Gøsta Esping-Andersen offered a typology of different types of welfare states, it was disturbing to see the UK ranked in the same category as the USA, largely on the basis of the meanness of its provision and its heavy reliance on market criteria to allocate resources.[23] That position has been reinforced in recent years. A series of recent reports have charted the rise of destitution in the

---

[21] D Porteous, 1783, *A letter to the citizens of Glasgow*, Glasgow: Chapman and Duncan, p 1.

[22] T Wontner, 1835, *Abolition of pauperism*, London: Steill, p 4.

[23] G Esping-Andersen, 1990, *The three worlds of welfare capitalism*, Cambridge: Polity.

UK – circumstances where people cannot afford to eat, keep warm or keep clean. Nearly two and a half million people in Britain went through that experience in 2019, before the pandemic.[24] The UN Special Rapporteur on Extreme Poverty and Human Rights comments:

> Policies of austerity introduced in 2010 continue largely unabated, despite the tragic social consequences. Close to 40 per cent of children are predicted to be living in poverty by 2021. Food banks have proliferated; homelessness and rough sleeping have increased greatly; tens of thousands of poor families must live in accommodation far from their schools, jobs and community networks; life expectancy is falling for certain groups; and the legal aid system has been decimated.[25]

If we were really concerned about human 'dignity', we might reasonably think that there is something undignified about having to sleep in a skip because one is living on the street,[26] or having to go to a food bank because there is not enough money for food.[27] That is Britain today.

The Poor Law and the welfare state

Some of the criticisms levelled at the welfare state start from the premise that it has become something much wider than originally planned. For example, we might read:

> The Left think that the welfare state was an avuncular arm placed around the entire nation from the cradle to the grave. But that is not what was intended – it was set up to help people help themselves and to provide a safety net for those who couldn't, or who found themselves in temporary difficulties either through illness or unemployment.[28]

---

[24] S Fitzpatrick, G Bramley, J Blenkinsopp, J Wood, F Sosenko, M Littlewood, S Johnsen, B Watts, M Treanor, J McIntyre, 2020, *Destitution in the UK 2020*, York: Joseph Rowntree Foundation, https://www.jrf.org.uk/report/destitution-uk-2020

[25] UN Human Rights Council, 2019, *Report of the Special Rapporteur on extreme poverty and human rights on his visit to the United Kingdom of Great Britain and Northern Ireland*, UN General Assembly A/HRC/41/39/Add.1, p 1.

[26] Biffa, 2020, New approach urgently required as risk of people sleeping in bins grows, https://www.biffa.co.uk/media-centre/news/new-approach-urgently-required-as-risk-of-people-sleeping-in-bins-grows

[27] Trussell Trust, 2020, Latest stats, https://www.trusselltrust.org/news-and-blog/latest-stats

[28] P Johnston, 2016, The destruction of welfarism is about liberation, not dependency, *Daily Telegraph*, 12 January.

Another critic tells us: 'A welfare system established to end privation and act as a safety net for those in difficulties has become all-pervasive.'[29] The idea that welfare was designed as a safety net, found in both these comments, is often repeated, but it is deeply, profoundly mistaken. A safety net system is there when all else fails. That was the sort of system we had before the welfare state. It is the model that the welfare state was supposed to replace.

The Poor Laws had made provision for the poorest people in society. The first national provisions, in 1598 and 1601, provided for a compulsory poor rate, levied by the parish; the creation of 'overseers' of relief; and provision for 'setting the poor on work'. In practice, there was no way to enforce a uniform national system, and there were marked differences in different places. Some parishes introduced workhouses – the workhouse at Abingdon, in 1631, was one of the first; some made the poor wear badges so that people would know who they were; some hired out paupers to local employers or farms. Workhouses became more common after an Act of 1723. A later Act in 1782, which stated that there should only be 'poorhouses', was not universally respected, and there were famous experiments with deterrent workhouses after 1815. The Poor Law Report of 1834 argued for a more coherent national system, and the Poor Law Amendment Act that followed set up the harsh, often punitive provisions which we have come to recognise from Dickens.

There were two key principles. One was the 'workhouse test': no relief should be issued outside the workhouse. The other was the principle of 'less eligibility': that the position of the pauper must always be less 'eligible', or less to be chosen, than the position of the independent labourer.[30] In practice, neither of these principles could be observed as strictly as their advocates hoped. Life in the workhouse could hardly be as bad as life outside them, unless – as happened in Andover[31] – the overseers were ready to let the inmates starve. The provision of medical services to the poor meant that some people who were not really destitute started to use the system, and the Poor Law authorities came to rely on the 'stigma of pauperism' as a deterrent.

However, the Poor Laws were, in many ways, the springboard from which other social services were developed. Part of the reason for this reflected the realisation, most notably in Edwin Chadwick's report on sanitary conditions,[32] that many of the problems that the Poor Law was dealing

---

[29] *Daily Telegraph*, 2015.

[30] S Checkland, O Checkland (eds), 1974, *The Poor Law report of 1834*, Harmondsworth: Penguin.

[31] I Anstruther, 1973, *The scandal of the Andover workhouse*, London: Geoffrey Bles.

[32] E Chadwick, 1842, *Report on the sanitary condition of the labouring population*, Edinburgh: Edinburgh University Press, 1965 edition.

with were the product of inadequate social arrangements; the scope of the Poor Law expanded in response to the pressures. Part was practical: the Guardians of the Poor were often the only local agencies available to do things. That is why they became responsible at first for public health, and then for many hospitals – the 'infirmaries'. But the loathing that the system inspired led to increasing attempts to make provision outside the scope of the Poor Law – among them old age pensions, school meals, medical insurance and – although it came to be just as mistrusted as the Poor Law itself – the 'dole', or means-tested provision for unemployment.

The Beveridge report, published in 1942, is often represented as the foundation of the welfare state.[33] It certainly became a symbol of what the Allies were fighting for, and it had an influence extending far past Britain. The report itself is not about the welfare state in its broadest sense. It's about social security – and more precisely, a plan for a system of national insurance, laid out in detail after the opening sections of the report. Social insurance, Beveridge explained, 'is an attack upon Want. But Want is one only of five giants on the road to reconstruction and in some ways the easiest to attack. The others are Disease, Ignorance, Squalor and Idleness'.[34] (The Five Giants are fabulously drawn in the wonderful cartoon by David Simonds, reproduced on the cover of this book.) His rhetoric proved, nonetheless, to be fundamental to the project. The welfare state was going to be a 'British revolution' – Beveridge's phrase.[35] It was going to cover people 'from the cradle to the grave'. That expression was not in the Beveridge report – Churchill used it in a wartime radio broadcast – but Beveridge tried to make it a reality: his 'universal' scheme included contribution classes for people who could not actually pay contributions, including pensioners and children.[36] He also specified three key 'assumptions' – a system of family allowances, a health service, and full employment – but he did not explain why they were necessary, or sketch out how they might be done.

The welfare state came into being on 5 July 1948, with a series of Acts covering health, social insurance, provision for children and welfare. (Two other significant measures, the introduction of universal secondary education and the commitment to full employment, had already been taken in 1944.) The welfare state was built, inevitably, on the foundation of services that had been laid before its inception – for example, the NHS inherited hospital buildings that had been built for a different era, including large numbers of long-stay institutions. However, the new system was clearly and explicitly intended to be a radical departure from what came before it. There were,

---

[33] Beveridge Report, 1942, *Social insurance and allied services*, Cmd 6404, London: HMSO.
[34] Beveridge Report, 1942, p 6.
[35] Beveridge Report, 1942, p 17.
[36] Beveridge Report, 1942, p 10.

historian Asa Briggs explained, three key elements. The welfare state would work:

> First by guaranteeing individuals and families a minimum income irrespective of the market value of their work, or their property. Second by narrowing the extent of insecurity by enabling individuals and families to meet certain 'social contingencies' (for example sickness, old age and unemployment) which lead otherwise to individual or family crisis, and third, by ensuring that all citizens without distinction of status or class are offered the best standards available in relation to a certain agreed range of social services.[37]

By 1948, Britain had travelled quite a long way from the idea that the welfare state was 'a system designed as a safety net for the most vulnerable'. The welfare state was going to be universal, for all citizens; it was going to be as good as it could be; and it was going to be delivered as of right. The difference between a service for everyone and a 'safety net' is sometimes described in terms of 'universality' and 'selectivity'. Universal services are delivered to everyone as of right; selective services make an assessment of means or needs, and delivered only to people who pass the test. These terms are properly seeking a description of the methods used, rather than a matter of general principle, and for that reason the literature of social policy is likely to draw a distinction between 'institutional' services, which in principle are intended for everyone, and 'residual' ones, which act as a safety net.[38] The health service is institutional, even if it does assess treatments according to people's needs; child protection is residual, because it only comes into play as a last resort, when bad things happen. Both are important.

The plan of the book

When people talk about 'welfare states', it could be a general way of speaking about the role of the state in the provision of social services; it could be about the organisation of welfare, regardless of who provides it – that is a more accurate way of thinking about the European 'welfare states'; and it could be about a political ideal. The British welfare state was the prime example of that third concept, even if it falls somewhat short in practice. The focus of this book falls squarely on the government and the state: the institutional arrangements, the services which the state provides, the policies which guide them, and the administrative processes by which

---

[37] A Briggs, 1961, The welfare state in historical perspective, *European Journal of Sociology*, 2(2), pp 228–30.

[38] H Wilensky, C Lebeaux, 1965, *Industrial society and social welfare*, New York: Free Press.

welfare is delivered. This is not a comprehensive study of social policy in Britain: that is a wider subject. Nor is it a study in the sociology of welfare. While a sociological perspective offers many insights to the examination of social policy, it is mainly relevant for understanding the social context and the outcomes for groups of people in society. Many of the issues which are of most interest to sociologists – race, class, gender, the family among them – are not the dimensions along which institutions and policies are formed, or services are delivered.

Conventionally, the British 'welfare state' is usually understood to be comprised of five main services: health, housing, social security, education and the 'personal social services', which mainly cover social care and child protection. The bulk of this book is addressed to the role of the state in relation to those services. I have made three modifications to the conventional agenda. One is about employment services, which are often seen as an adjunct to social security provision. The second is the relatively new field of 'equalities', which in common with the other social services now has both an institutional structure and a framework of national policy. The third is the range of public services, such as roads, parks, libraries and rescue services, which work on similar principles to the social services.

Within that range of topics, the areas I have mainly focussed on are broadly defined, but the details matter. This book is concerned with what used to be called social administration – engaging with the 'how' of policy, not just the 'why'. Taking a long view, the issues typically reflect the impact of major reforms taken some time ago. In the case of health care, for example, there have been repeated attempts to inject competition and market principles; in social security, there has been 'welfare reform' and Universal Credit; in social care, there is individualised budgeting and self-directed support, a set of policies which have been previously tried under different guises; in housing policy, the continued pursuit of 'affordability'. None of these was part of the original conception of the welfare state, but the welfare state has never been static. In each of the services, there has been a long series of reforms, and some of the arguments I am reviewing go back thirty or forty years, some even longer. For example, I know that some people will think it odd that I have spent more time discussing a 1962 circular on social care than on the Dilnot Commission's report on funding the system;[39] but the circular has guided policy for almost sixty years, and the Dilnot recommendations for 'urgent and lasting' reform have never been implemented. While I have been concerned with the practicalities of service delivery, I have not devoted much attention to some recurring issues considered in many regular, up-to-date reports from the services: managing expenditure, recruiting and

---

[39] Commission on Funding of Care and Support, 2011, *Fairer care funding*, https://tinyurl.com/yy85jbrf

training staff or developing digital technology. Nor have I tried to cost or plan specific reforms; it is not that sort of book. In every case, I have been thinking about where the services have gone wrong, and what they need to do to get things right.

The defenders of the 'welfare state' start at a disadvantage. The people who want to attack welfare have bigger guns. Most of the press in the UK is determinedly right-wing; there is an ever-flowing stream of neoliberal propaganda about the benefits of laissez-faire and markets, and the evils of collective provision. There may be some legitimate criticisms to be made, but lots of the accusations are off-beam. I will not be able to deal with all the objections – if I did, the book would largely be consumed by them – but I will need to clear the fog.

It does not help that there is a lot of misleading stuff out there, from supporters as well as opponents. Many people believe, quite passionately and sincerely, that the policies they are following are the right ones – there are examples in every chapter of this book. Part of the task is to repair the damage caused by botched or ill-conceived reforms. Personalisation in social care has been falling short for thirty years,[40] but people are still convinced that the policy ought to work, if only it was applied with more confidence and a deeper purse. 'Active' employment policies have been pursued, intermittently, for forty years; they have become progressively more directive and more punitive, despite the evidence that this is counter-productive.[41] Using benefits to pay for the costs of renting, instead of paying for housing directly, has been the policy for nearly fifty years. As I will explain, the 'personalisation' that goes with social care is scarcely personal; social security is not about getting people into work; and housing policy will not get anywhere if we spend all our time talking about tenure and affordability.

The chapters in this book largely follow a common pattern. I begin with a short description of the field of policy, and the institutional arrangements that have been made in that field. I have identified some positive trends, but otherwise I have sought to dismiss the distractions and false trails that blight the discussion of welfare. And then I try to re-focus the debate on the issues which actually matter. People who want to defend the welfare state, as I do, usually want to criticise the welfare state, too, because if they don't nothing will ever improve. That is the main aim of the book: to think about ways of doing things better.

---

[40] P Spicker, 2013, Personalisation falls short, *British Journal of Social Work*, 43(7), pp 1259–75.

[41] B Watts, S Fitzpatrick, 2018, *Welfare conditionality*, Abingdon: Routledge.

2

Social security

Social security benefits cover a huge range of different circumstances. The most important are pensions, provision for disability, meeting housing costs and helping people on low incomes, but there are lots of others. In some minds, benefits are there to save people from poverty, but that is only true of some benefits, and not the largest part. Other benefits are there to help people meet personal needs, some to protect people undergoing major changes, and some to support specific activities such as child care and social care. There are many possible objectives: for example, meeting needs, responding to emergencies, economic management, compensation, redistribution and social inclusion.

Most of the services that I will be discussing in this book operate by providing people with something – for example, medical care, housing or schooling. Social security, by contrast, is paid in cash, rather than in kind. That means it is not like other social services. It works by transferring money to people to spend, and the things they buy – such as food, fuel and clothing – are then up to them. It follows that benefit recipients are expected to use the money to buy things from commercial providers. Social security is not a way of making public provision: it is a way of enabling people to pay for private provision. Some political commentators, the radical right or 'neoliberals', believe that commercial markets are a much better way of managing resources than public provision of goods and services can ever be.[1] I will be examining some other aspects of those arguments in due course, but for present purposes I want only to note the relationship of that position to social security policy. It is implicit in any call for better social security that the market is expected to provide – and so, that commercial markets work. If people are short of food – many people are[2] – that is usually taken to be an argument for getting them more money, not for bigger food banks.

The right-wing argument for market-based provision is not an argument for services to be cut, though that often overshadows anything else the neoliberals have to say. It is an argument for social security to be paid instead of providing social services.[3] If we wanted people to buy things they do not

---

[1] For example, M Friedman, R Friedman, 1981, *Free to choose*, Harmondsworth: Penguin.
[2] H Lambie-Mumford, 2019, The growth of food banks in Britain and what they mean for social policy, *Critical Social Policy*, 39(1), pp 3–22.
[3] For example, A Seldon, 1977, *Charge!*, London: Temple Smith.

currently have to pay for, such as medical care or schooling, they would need to have the money to do it. That shift happened in housing policy: as the subsidies for council housing were withdrawn, governments were obliged to offer benefits for housing costs instead, because otherwise most people who were in council housing could not have afforded anywhere to live. Conversely, if we feel that certain goods and services are so important that people should have them regardless – for example, child care, medical prescriptions or an internet connection – it may well be that social security is not the best way to obtain them. Of these examples, child care is currently dealt with partly through the social security system, and partly through education services; prescriptions are treated differently in different countries of the UK; the internet is not provided for. There is a reasonable case for more things to be taken out of the market – such as social care, burial and cremation, or public transport (often free for pensioners, but not for others). I return to that argument later, in Chapter 10.

The benefit system

There are several main types of social security benefit.

- *Insurance benefits*, such as State Pension, depend on the contributions that people make over a period of time.
- *Means-tested benefits* are based on the level of income that people have. This covers two types:
  - minimum income benefits, which guarantee a minimum income for people who fall below an income threshold; and
  - tapered benefits, which offer an amount that is gradually withdrawn as income increases.
- *Non-means-tested benefits* select people on the basis of a test of need: the main examples are Personal Independence Payment (PIP) and Attendance Allowance, both for people with disabilities.
- *Universal benefits* have no test of contribution, means or needs. The best known is Child Benefit. Its coverage has been compromised by clawback through the tax system, but the central mechanism is still universal: it is a categorical, long-term benefit paid in respect of all children, without being subject to other tests. (The principle of universality is discussed further in Chapter 10.)
- *Discretionary benefits* make it possible to offer some financial support in unusual circumstances: local welfare assistance (and national schemes in Scotland and Wales) works this way.

For more than fifty years, until at least the 1990s, the Beveridge scheme provided the backbone of the benefits system. The bulk of the money, for pensioners, unemployed people and sickness, was provided on the basis of contributions. Gradually, however, means-testing came to be more and more important, as the gaps in the Beveridge system became apparent. Little thought was given at first to the basic means-tested benefit, National Assistance, which brought people's income to a minimum level; it was mainly there to mop up the few cases who wouldn't otherwise be covered. It was re-christened Supplementary Benefit in the 1960s, and by the late 1970s it had come to deal with more than five million people; it was renamed Income Support as part of reviews in the 1980s. Like Universal Credit, its modern successor, it provided for housing costs, and long-term sickness; unlike Universal Credit, it also covered the positions of pensioners and owner-occupiers. (It did not cover low pay; that was first done in 1971, with Family Income Supplement, which became Family Credit, then Tax Credits, and then part of Universal Credit.) National Assistance, Supplementary Benefit and Income Support were means-tested benefits, all working on the same principle: they guaranteed a minimum income. If people's income was less than the (very low) threshold, these benefits would make up the difference. This principle still applies for pensioners, who can receive Pension Credit, but it has been abandoned for families and people of working age.

Housing Benefit, Tax Credits and now Universal Credit are also means-tested, but they work on a different principle from minimum income benefits: they are tapered according to income, and they are gradually withdrawn as other income increases. The design of tapered benefits has the advantage that people do not lose all their entitlements because of a small increase in income. However, because of the way that these benefits work, people on higher incomes but with greater liabilities may have a higher benefit entitlement than people who start with less. They also have a notable practical disadvantage: claimants do not know what they are entitled to, or when they cease to be entitled. The shift to tapered benefits has sounded a death-knell for the idea that there is a safety net or minimum income that people can be sure of receiving. Universal Credit does not guarantee a minimum: there are long delays in receiving it, lengthy sanctions for non-compliance with commands, and important exclusions. There are also limits on the benefit that can be received, limits on the number of children who will be supported, and substantial deductions for previous overpayments or debts, which all imply that claimants will receive less than they are deemed to need. Donald Hirsch comments on

> the lack of any empirical link between support levels and need; the inconsistent treatment of different groups; and the exclusion of particular households or groups from a basic level of support ... the UK's 'safety-net' benefits, which have never maintained a systematic

link with subsistence, have recently become both less adequate and more arbitrary in terms of enabling claimants to make ends meet at some basic level.[4]

The growth of means-testing has come about partly because of a belief that the best way to use benefits is to increase the income of people who have least, and partly because of a conviction that targeting the poorest must be the best way to use scarce resources. Those would be powerful reasons, if only means-testing worked as it should. Unfortunately, the process is beset with problems. Some of the difficulties are problems that bedevil any selective service: knowing who to include and who to exclude, making sure that the people who are supposed to get the benefit actually do get it, and trying to make sure that the outcomes are fair. This applies as much to benefits that rely on a test of need, such as PIP or Attendance Allowance, as it does to means-tested benefits: in both types of benefit, the qualifying conditions are complex and difficult to negotiate, and there are notorious failures of coverage and take-up. But then means-testing, beyond that, presents a series of practical problems. There ought to be a practical and fair way of taking resources into account. Capital and savings have to be considered – this has been a major problem in the course of the current pandemic. Income is not a fixed, or even a long-term, feature of most people's lives: it can change unpredictably, day by day, week by week, month by month. People on a low income often have irregular incomes; some could double or halve in a three-month period.[5] The rules of the benefit system frequently resort to 'notional', 'deemed', assumed or attributed incomes or capital, because finding and processing the genuine details is so difficult. Information needs to be managed, and managed rapidly – the Universal Credit system was supposed to do this in 'real time', but the effect of trying to adjust benefits in line with fluctuating incomes has been to offer support that is irregular, unstable and unpredictable.[6]

Thinking differently about benefits

Debates about social security policy are riddled with misconceptions. I cannot deal with them all here – there is a longer discussion in my book, *What's wrong with social security benefits?*[7] – but there are two in particular I think I need to anticipate. The first is about social security spending, which

[4] D Hirsch, 2020, After a decade of austerity, does the UK have a safety net worth its name? in J Rees, M Pomati, E Heins (eds) *Social policy review 32*, Bristol: Policy Press.
[5] J Hills, 2015, *Good times, bad times*, Bristol: Policy Press, ch 4 and p 107.
[6] House of Lords Economic Affairs Committee, 2020, *Universal Credit isn't working*, HL 105.
[7] P Spicker, 2017, *What's wrong with social security benefits?*, Bristol: Policy Press.

is one of the biggest elements in the government accounts. The figures are large – as more than five million people claim the basic disability benefits, a miserly £1 a week on those benefits would cost more than £250 million. They are often confusingly presented. For example, some of the figures quoted in the press include civil service pensions; they have much more in common with private occupational pensions, which are not counted, than they do with State Pensions. The main expenditure on benefits is made by two agencies, which are the Department for Work and Pensions (DWP) and Her Majesty's Revenue and Customs (HMRC); with the introduction of Universal Credit, the responsibility for Tax Credits is gradually being shifted into the remit of the DWP. There is some other expenditure at the local authority level, but most of that is accounted for within the DWP budget. The pre-pandemic forecast for 2020/2021 was that benefit expenditure would come to £223.5 billion.[8]

It is worth thinking for a moment about what 'government spending' is supposed to mean in this context. If the government spends money on building a hospital and buying medicines, it can reasonably be said to have 'spent' the money. If it puts the money into pensions or unemployment benefits, it has not actually 'spent' the money at all; it has passed the money to the pensioners or unemployed people to spend. In economic terms, benefits are 'transfer payments' – they shift money from some people to other people. The amount of money there is in the economy remains just the same. If transfers were to make a difference to the way the economy works, it would have to be because the people who were receiving the money went on to act differently from the people who had the money to begin with. That might be true to some degree – we expect people on low incomes to spend proportionately more on food than richer people do, to save less, and to spend less abroad – but those effects are fairly marginal in economic terms.[9] (It follows that there is a reasonable case for accounting for transfer payments differently from other public expenditure. That would make more sense than the current situation; it should help policy-makers to understand what benefits are actually doing, and it would get some half-baked economic objections out of the way. However, changing the way the payments appear in the accounts would make no immediate difference to people's living standards, which means that it is probably not a point that would command much political support.)

The second set of misconceptions relate to what benefits are supposed to do. Looking at what the benefits system mainly does, as opposed to

[8] Department of Work and Pensions, 2020, Benefit expenditure and caseload tables 2020, summary table; plus Non-DWP welfare, from DWP Spring Statement 2019.
[9] J Ostry, A Berg, C Tsangarides, 2014, *Redistribution, inequality and growth*, Washington, DC: International Monetary Fund, http://www.imf.org/external/pubs/ft/sdn/2014/sdn1402.pdf

what people imagine it does, the roles which call for the largest amounts of money are these:

- Providing a secure but partial basic income, that can be combined with other sources of income. This is done, for example, by the State Pension and Child Benefit. Looking at what social security provision does well, these benefits are the prime examples; and these two benefits alone account for £113 billion, half the total spend. Child Benefit does not meet all the needs of children, by some way, but it is an important, stable part of the income of most families. State Pensions, equally, do not meet the all the needs of pensioners; nor are they meant to. Most pensioners already have some income that is not provided from their State Pension – about two-thirds of pensioners now have some occupational pension.
- Income support. Supporters of the benefit system often suppose that benefits are focused on poverty; that is not quite right. The main protection that the system offers against poverty lies in its general coverage, not in those residual benefits that are specifically addressed to low income. In due course, Universal Credit will mainly serve three main groups: people with long-term sickness or incapacity, people working on low incomes, and people who are unemployed; there are still legacy benefits for these contingencies. Pensioners on lower incomes can get Pension Credit. In so far as income support can be taken to deal with poverty, it is because the circumstances where it is necessary, including retirement, may well lead to poverty otherwise; but low income is not necessarily the deciding factor in eligibility.
- Offering people supplementary incomes in recognition of special needs. This is the main function of disability benefits. Disability benefits are not intended to cover the extra costs of disability,[10] because there is nothing in the process of claiming the benefits that relates to those costs. Nor do they meet social care needs (as the Barker report on social care supposed)[11] – if they did, they would have to provide vastly more money. The main purpose of Attendance Allowance was never to pay for attendance; it was always intended to supplement the general income of people with disabilities, because they would suffer lower incomes throughout their lives.[12] These benefits work less well than universal benefits, because qualification is complex and take-up is not good, but they have something

---

[10] Department for Work and Pensions, 2017, *Equality analysis: PIP assessment criteria*, p 4, https://www.gov.uk/government/uploads/system/uploads/attachment_data/file/593392/pip-assessment-criteria-equality-analysis.pdf

[11] K Barker (Chair), 2014, *A new settlement for health and social care*, London: King's Fund.

[12] A Morris MP, 1970, in *Hansard*, 10 and 15 July.

in common with benefits providing a secure basic income: they have to be seen in combination with other sources of income.

- Providing the resources for people to pay for certain key items. The largest example is Housing Benefit, but there are other much smaller benefits which are meant to deal with similar issues, such as Funeral Payments, free prescriptions and school uniform grants. (Help with the expenses of residential care used to be done through social security, but this responsibility was passed to local authorities as part of the Griffiths reforms.)

A long series of government documents have presented the primary purpose of benefits for people of working age as being to encourage people out of unemployment.[13] Most benefits have little to do with employment and the world of work – they are addressed to other issues entirely – and unemployment as such generally represents a limited proportion of all claims. However, the belief that benefits ought to focus on work is so strong that a huge institutional edifice has been constructed around it. I will come back to services relating to employment in another chapter, but we ought to understand that the focus on work is woefully misplaced.

Dealing with complex rules

The social security system is rule-bound. That is both a virtue and a vice: a virtue, because rules are there to make services regular and predictable, and a vice, because the rules become progressively more complicated whenever difficult and thorny issues come up. So, we get special rules for migrants, for services in social housing, for people who have no settled way of life, for ex-prisoners, for people fleeing domestic violence, and so on – the list of contingencies is inexhaustible. The rules governing social security have grown inexorably. Some benefits have been excised – Death Grants and Maternity Grants were both part of the Beveridge scheme – but even when a benefit is being replaced, as currently Disability Living Allowance (DLA) is being replaced by PIP, and Housing Benefit is being absorbed into the great blob of Universal Credit, the established ways of doing things carry on.

Benefits have to be complex, but often they are made more complex by the accretion of additional rules. Conditionality is the imposition of moral rules designed to punish or exclude 'undeserving' cases, and to enforce compliance. It commonly takes the form of behavioural requirements, monitoring and surveillance of benefit recipients, and sanctions for

---

[13] DWP, 2007, *In work, better off*, Cm 7130; DWP, 2010, *21st century welfare*, Cm 7913; DWP, 2010, *Universal Credit: welfare that works*, Cm 7957; DWP, 2018, *Universal Credit programme full business case summary*.

non-compliance.[14] The vast majority of sanctions that have been imposed under Universal Credit have been for failure to come to a meeting.[15]

Benefits often interact with each other, making levels of entitlement unclear. Benefits and income cover incompatible periods, making payments unpredictable. Some of the rules that have been developed in social security are arcane. Here are two small examples of what claimants are up against, from the excellent Child Poverty Action Group Handbook:

> Some income may be treated as capital, and some capital treated as income.[16]

> Your maximum guarantee credit is known as the appropriate minimum guarantee and is made up of the standard minimum guarantee, and, where applicable, additional amounts ... Your appropriate minimum guarantee may be reduced in certain circumstances.[17]

So income is capital, capital is income, the maximum is the minimum, and the minimum can be reduced. Go figure. The process by which rules are arrived at is often that a particular case has been identified, a judgment has to be made, and this judgment is then enshrined in the rules. We may find, among other examples, specific rules regarding the treatment of pensioner couples who move to the same care home, the treatment of grants from Sports UK or the management of backdated pay rises when a person is receiving parental or adoption pay. The rules are what they are. There is no way to discern what they might be by reason, guesswork or common sense.

Too many people can't make sense of what benefits are meant to do. They can't tell whether they might be entitled, and lots of people who are entitled don't receive them.[18] Currently, for example, people who get PIP might have part of their entitlement from a 'care component', part from a mobility component – but there used to be separate benefits for mobility and for care. It appears that many of the people who apply have no reasonable prospect of receiving the benefit, and the DWP commissioned research into DLA, which PIP is based on, to try to find out what they were thinking of. The research found that many of the applicants simply didn't understand what the benefit is for. They tended to see it as a top-up to Employment

---

[14] B Watts, S Fitzpatrick, 2018, *Welfare conditionality*, Abingdon: Routledge.

[15] D Webster, 2020, *Briefing: Benefit sanctions statistics*, Child Poverty Action Group, June, pp 11–12.

[16] Child Poverty Action Group, 2021, *Welfare benefits and tax credits handbook 2021/2022*, London: CPAG, p 409.

[17] CPAG, 2021, pp 263–4.

[18] See, for example, DWP, 2016, *Income related benefits: estimates of takeup 2014/15*, https://www.gov.uk/government/statistics/income-related-benefits-estimates-of-take-up.

and Support Allowance, and typically they applied because they thought that they might as well have a crack at it.[19] By contrast, the people who should get this support don't know to claim. The best estimates are that somewhere between 50% and 70% of the people entitled get the mobility component, and only something like 30% to 50% of those entitled get the care component.[20]

Benefits could be simplified to some degree by stripping away some of the clutter, but a fundamental problem remains. 'Personalisation', the idea that benefits can be tailored to the needs of the individual, has generally been pursued by trying to make the benefits more sensitive to differences in individual circumstances. That is based on the breathtakingly arrogant presumption, that the system is capable of managing all the information this would require. Many benefits demand a huge amount of personal information from the claimants, and it is not information that they necessarily can supply. Asking about income is an obvious problem; it's not too difficult to do if people have a single source of regular income, but that is not the way of the world. Many people do not know what their income will be in the next four weeks. They may be owed money they have earned, but have no idea when it will appear. But the problems are not just about money. Some do not know if they have work. They are not always sure whether or not they have a partner, or who lives where – there are often long periods of uncertainty before people form a relationship, and again when the relationship is breaking up. Fully three-quarters of people with disabilities either do not know if they are disabled, or say they are disabled 'sometimes'.[21]

The benefits which are most successful, the State Pension and Child Benefit, have in common that they are granted for very long periods, and that, once granted, entitlement doesn't change much if at all. The benefits which are least successful ask for a staggering amount of detail. Take, for example, Funeral Payments, which ask for details about the resources of the deceased person, the personal circumstances and resources of the applicant, the relationship of the applicant to the deceased person, the arrangements that have been made for the funeral, and the relationship of other people to the deceased person who might otherwise have been expected to meet the expenses. There are just too many moving parts for this to be manageable.

The process of simplification has often been taken to mean that benefits should be more like each other – for example, making common rules on

---

[19] A Thomas, 2008, *Disability Living Allowance: disallowed claims*, London: DWP, p 20.

[20] D Kasparova, A Marsh, D Wilkinson, 2007, *The takeup rate of Disability Living Allowance and Attendance Allowance: feasibility study*, London: Department for Work and Pensions.

[21] UK Department for Work and Pensions, 2013, *Ad hoc statistics of disability, from the ONS Opinions and Lifestyle Survey*, https://www.gov.uk/government/publications/disability-statistics-from-the-ons-opinions-and-lifestyle-survey-January-to-march-2013

capital, or subjecting recipients who are too sick to work to a requirement to be ready for work. There is a similar rationale behind the idea of unifying benefits; but lumping benefits together does not make them simpler. The unification of Housing Benefit, which brought together Rent Rebate, Rent Allowance and some of the provisions made as part of Income Support, was described in its day as the greatest fiasco in the history of the welfare state[22] – there have been a few contenders since. Universal Credit has brought together unemployment, incapacity, disability, low pay, child support and housing costs. The Child Poverty Action Group has proposed (and costed) a series of improvements to the system, such as cutting the delay in first payment, scrapping the two-child limit and the benefit cap, and increasing benefit rates.[23] I would not demur from any of them; it is important to do what we can to make people's lives better now, rather than focusing on distant uplands. We should understand, however, that Universal Credit will never work as intended. It has failed extensively, both in the aims that were set for it – simplification, economy, engagement with work, and reduction of error – and the aims that should have been set for it, such as adequacy, accessibility and security of income. The sheer size of the system, the varied needs it has to deal with, and the lack of responsiveness that is built into a uniform national system, has meant that – so far at least – it has fallen short at every level. It is difficult to understand, hard to access, administratively cumbersome, penal and imposes tests on people that have little relevance to their situation. It combines, in one benefit, just about every major element of the benefit system that is known not to work.[24]

The call for simplification is also the reasoning behind many arguments for a 'Citizens Basic Income', which – unlike Universal Credit – would be unconditional, not means-tested and paid to every person. This is a much better idea than Universal Credit, but it still runs in to a familiar set of problems. I have yet to see a Basic Income scheme which engages with the practical issues that confront benefits schemes everywhere – such as whether non-citizens will be included, whether people will have to claim and how, how payments will be made, what happens when people move house, what happens to people with very limited capacity, how overpayments are dealt with, who gets payments destined for children, how to stop creditors seizing the benefit, or what happens when someone dies.[25] There are, however,

---

[22] *The Times*, cited in R Walker, 1986, Aspects of administration, in P Kemp (ed) *The future of housing benefits*, Glasgow: Centre for Housing Research, p 39.

[23] Child Poverty Action Group, 2021, *Universal Credit: what needs to change?*, https://cpag. org.uk/policy-and-campaigns/briefing/universal-credit-what-needs-change-make-it-fit-children-and-families

[24] Spicker, 2017, p 55.

[25] See P Spicker, 2019, *Some reservations about Basic Income*, Glasgow: Scottish Universities Insight Unit.

more fundamental objections. If a Citizens Basic Income were to be paid for by replacing existing benefits, as most of the schemes suggest, it would do little for most people on low incomes. Simplicity implies less sensitivity to individual circumstances, and unless the scheme is extraordinarily generous, some people are going to be worse off. All the Basic Income schemes that have been proposed have losers as well as winners.[26] Beyond that, many of the claims made for a Basic Income – that it will be transformative, liberating and conquer poverty – are over-optimistic. Money can do a lot, but it cannot do everything.

Reforming benefits

Social security systems in different countries are generally compared, not by looking at the technicalities or the purposes of different benefits, but at the 'income package' – the combination of income from different sources which delivers a regular income. Income is, in the jargon, 'fungible'; it can always be mixed in with other income, and once that happens the different types of income are indistinguishable from each other. It follows that securing a core basic income, the primary objective of most of the money devoted to benefits, is not necessarily the same thing as providing an adequate income outright.

To be effective, benefits need to reduce the insecurity that people experience. They should aim to deliver predictable, regular amounts of income. They need to slow down the rate at which they are adjusted to changing circumstance, and they should be less conditional. They should not all stop at once if things go wrong. The benefits need to be straightforward, to reduce the number of mistakes that are made: for example, benefits should always disregard income from other benefits. And they should have clearer, more sharply defined roles. The way to deliver benefits that make sense from the point of view of the person who receives them is to have benefits with a clear meaning and purpose; and the best way to take account of individual differences is not to fine-tune the rules of every benefit, but to have a range of benefits that can be delivered in different combinations, without complicating things by interacting with other benefits, or with each other. In France, that general approach is followed, with one important additional feature: nearly all benefits are paid on the same day of the month. People get different packages of income, but the delivery is predictable.

We need, then, to consider how income packages can be improved, and that implies not a uniform benefit structure, but a range of benefits that can be combined in different ways. Begin with pensioners. There is a particular case to reconsider the position of pensioners in the bottom third of the

---

[26] M Torry, 2018, *Why we need a Citizen's Income*, Bristol: Policy Press.

income distribution, the people who currently receive or ought to receive Pension Credit, though many do not actually get it. One option would be to make the State Pension more universal. Pensioners retiring since 2016 do not, in most cases, get the earnings-related element of the State Pension, S2P; instead, there is a relatively simple mechanism, called COPE or the Contracted-Out Pension Equivalent, which means in practice that the earnings-related element is not paid when an occupational pension is available. That sets an interesting precedent. The justification for COPE is supposedly that people's entitlement depends on the contributions they have made, but the distributive effect has been to target resources on pensioners with lower incomes, without requiring a complicated means-test. A universal benefit that is subject to the existence of an occupational pension, but otherwise unconditional, would benefit two-thirds of people of pension age, and particularly benefit the third on the lowest incomes, giving many pensioners a more secure income with better coverage than Pension Credit does.

For families, there is already an (almost) universal option in Child Benefit, and the starting point should be to increase that. Families with younger children tend to have lower incomes, mainly because their mothers are less able to participate in the labour market, or are disadvantaged. That could also justify an extra payment for children aged 0–3, because families with younger children tend to be on lower incomes – that could be bundled into Child Benefit, but equally it could be done by way of a separate benefit. Another possibility might be to revive One Parent Benefit, because lone parents are so often disadvantaged: the main catch with that is that it implies a test to establish who is a lone parent, and that in turn implies a test of who is cohabiting.

A different set of examples might provide further benefits for people with disabilities, currently mainly protected by PIP or Attendance Allowance, and by means-tested benefits for people on low incomes. There has to be some way of distinguishing people who do have disabilities from people who don't. That implies that there will be a test of need, but it doesn't have to be done by the present system of assessment. Some benefits might be introduced to offer support for particular disadvantages: terminal illness, no-fault compensation for accidents, a heating allowance for people with disabilities, or support into education. A mobility allowance might be revived: we used to have one, but it was folded into other benefits (currently it is part of PIP) whose purpose is complex and puzzling to claimants. Some benefits could be awarded simply for having certain medically verifiable conditions: a Blind Persons Allowance, major neurological disorders, payments for loss of a limb or organ (currently allowed for in Industrial Injuries Benefits and War Pensions, but not more generally). Treating these as separate benefits would imply that some people might be able to claim more than one benefit, if they qualified for more than one; to which the obvious rejoinder is, why not? They would act, as disability benefits were originally intended to act, to form part of an income package for a broad group of people whose incomes are otherwise liable to be depressed throughout their lives.

For others there could be a lump-sum supplement. If we want benefits to be 'targeted' without the creation of massive bureaucracy, the supplements could be triggered by, and attached to, the receipt of other benefits. The current models, which demonstrate that this is feasible, are the Winter Fuel payment and the Xmas bonus. If we can do it once a year, we can do it two, three or four times.

These ideas are certainly practical, because they are all based on existing administrative mechanisms. There are three common objections, two of which can be dismissed easily. One is that they're not fair, because only some people will benefit and others won't. Why help blind people and not people with cancer? That question reflects a long-standing debate between disability advocacy groups, but it's a very weak argument: complaining that some people in need shouldn't get a benefit, because others don't, does not take account of anyone's needs, and that cannot be better than responding to some people at least. A second objection is that this would all be better done in one big benefit. That is a recipe for confusion and incomplete coverage; it is much easier for people to recognise that a benefit is meant for them if it refers clearly and directly to their position. The third, more serious concern is that new benefits would call for a lot of money that otherwise might legitimately be used for other purposes. The advantage of defining benefits and contingencies more specifically and closely is that it becomes possible to identify just what the expected costs should be. However, there is always an 'opportunity cost' – some other way the money might have been used. Whether any of this is worth doing is a matter for political judgment.

Whatever we do, social security is going to be complex. Benefits are intended to do many things: sometimes to offer a minimum income, possibly to smooth people's incomes, to encourage people into the labour market, to include people in society, to change their behaviour, to help government manage the economy. They are responding to a wide range of different needs: among them, old age, disability, unemployment, low pay, sickness, bereavement and caring. There are circumstances where we offer benefits for so that people will be able to pay for specific items: housing costs, child care, winter fuel, funerals. The system of benefits deals with too many people, and too many circumstances, to manage everything all at once. It may be tempting, at times, to look for ways to cut corners, but cutting corners means that some people will be run over. It helps to think small. Money is money; little benefits mix with other income to make up incomes in different ways.

The complexity has to be recognised and managed; but to do that, governments have to lower their sights, not to make the system more complicated still. I have previously argued the case in these terms: 'No system can operate for millions of people while attempting to subject the individuals within it to a detailed scrutiny of their circumstances, conduct and merits. Benefits need to assume less, demand less and work with less.'[27]

Social security	
Key points	Social security provides money, to be spent in a commercial market.
	Money can be brought together from different sources. It doesn't have to be done by one benefit.
	Social security is provided for many reasons, but its main purpose is to provide some secure income.
Positive developments	Most of the cost of social security currently consists of benefits offering a secure but only partial contribution towards income. Earnings-related pensions, Child Benefit and benefits for disability were all developed after the welfare state's foundation.
Where policy has gone wrong	Some degree of selectivity is necessary, but the process is liable to fail in some cases and to leave gaps in others.
	Lumping benefits together doesn't make them simpler.
	Benefits don't have much to do with work. Tying social security to employment services has been to the detriment of both.
What to do instead	A secure income can have many components. The benefits package can be made of smaller, more specific benefits.
	Benefits need to be less conditional, and more predictable. More could be universal.

[27] Spicker, 2017, p 113.

3

The National Health Service

The National Health Service is held in some high regard, and with considerable affection. People love it for the high principles it embodies, the protection and security it offers and (for the most part) their experience of its service – there are few families where no one has experienced a serious illness. The NHS is, a former Conservative chancellor famously observed, 'the closest thing the English people have to a religion'.[1] The rationale for the NHS is both moral – it represents a moral commitment and a right to welfare for everyone in the community – and practical. The service has been, for most, the very model of the welfare state – a universal service, free to all at the point of delivery.

Despite that, it has also been the subject of continual criticism. The criticism has abated during the coronavirus crisis, but there is no reason to expect that it will be quelled for the next few years. Some part of the criticism has been based in a loss of respect for the expertise of the medical profession, evidenced partly in press reports about failures, and partly by the increasing numbers of cases taken against doctors and health trusts for negligence or malpractice. Some part, too, has been political. Since the 1960s, there has been a steady stream of commentators ready to say that it could all be done better if only more was done through the private sector.[2] And part, perhaps, is intrinsic to the nature of the NHS. The NHS, the Prime Minister has said, is 'powered by love'. That, the *Economist* comments, is genuinely true, some of the time: 'but it can also run on anger'.[3] Enoch Powell, a former Minister of Health, wrote nearly sixty years ago that everyone in the NHS had an interest in saying that it wasn't good enough, because that was the way to get better funding. A private firm tends to attract business by claiming that the service it provides is wonderful, even if it is on the brink of collapse. The NHS, by contrast, rewards 'shroud waving' – showing how awful the consequences of underfunding can be. Powell commented:

---

[1] Cited in R Murray, 2018, *From Margaret Thatcher to Theresa May: 30 years of the public's views about the NHS and public spending*, King's Fund, https://www.kingsfund.org.uk/blog/2018/02/30-years-public-views-nhs-public-spending

[2] For example, T Worstall, 2014, *How to fix the NHS: privatisation*, Adam Smith Institute, https://www.adamsmith.org/blog/uncategorized/how-to-fix-the-nhs-privatisation; K Niemitz, 2016, *Universal health care without the NHS*, London: Institute of Economic Affairs.

[3] *The Economist*, 2021, Hands on, 13 February, pp 22–3.

One of the most striking features of the National Health Service is the continual, deafening chorus of complaint which rises day and night from every part of it, a chorus only interrupted when someone suggests that a different system altogether might be preferable ... The universal Exchequer financing of the service endows everyone providing as well as using it with a vested interest in denigrating it.[4]

On occasion, media coverage of the NHS seems to imply that it has been slow to reform and modernise, and that it has hardly changed since its foundation in 1948. For example, the reforms introduced in 2012 were 'arguably the biggest restructuring the NHS had seen in its 63 year history'.[5] But the NHS has changed constantly during its long life. Some of those changes have been heavily publicised; others have not. In the most visible changes, the NHS has passed through a long, labyrinthine series of administrative reforms. In the early 1970s, the Conservative government arranged for the NHS to be run by administrators, rather than medical staff, reasoning that it would make much more sense to give administration to people who cost less and knew what they were doing. In the mid-1970s, the emphasis fell heavily on planning, co-operation and joint working. The health services and local government had both been reformed and given responsibility for common geographical areas; joint finance and planning created openings for the development of services, such as services for learning disability, that had received too little attention. Less than ten years later, however, another Conservative government started to unpick the reforms introduced by its predecessor. The Griffiths reforms of the early 1980s (not to be confused with the later reforms of social care, which followed another Griffiths report) introduced the principles of the 'new public management' – the introduction of agencies, the encouragement of multiple providers, management by objectives and target-setting. Further administrative reforms in the 1990s, with experiments relating to 'commissioning' services, led to the idea of an 'internal market'. The providers – health service professionals and administrators – were faced with a huge degree of administrative certainty. Many responded by using the techniques of the 1970s – collaborative partnership working. From that, ideas like general practice partnerships and 'clinical commissioning groups' were to emerge.

The Labour government formally abandoned the idea of the internal market, but it kept most of its elements in place, and made the emphasis on target-setting even stronger. The administrative authorities were replaced, at first gradually and then at pace, by 'trusts'. Then the Coalition government presided over a further reform, designed to make the NHS more like a

---

[4] J E Powell, 1963, *Medicine and politics*, London: Pitman Medical.
[5] N Seddon, 2012, NHS reforms caught in the act, *British Medical Journal*, 345(7866) 38.

market than ever – aiming to establish multiple purchasers, multiple providers and the use of monetary values as a reference point. This has been seen by many critics as a covert route to privatisation,[6] but if so, it has been a long, slow process.[7] The current Conservative government, while having no open reservations about private care, plans to roll that back even that much, restoring control to ministers.[8] (Depending on how you count them, that may prove to be the fifth large-scale organisational reform of the NHS introduced by Conservative governments.) I am going to discuss other issues about markets and privatisation elsewhere in this book, but it does not get to the nub of the issues, any more than discussing the institutional structures does.

If we focus instead on some of the less widely commented issues, the process of reform starts to look very different. Begin with one of the most radical changes in the NHS's history – radical not in the sense of being sudden, but of fundamentally changing the character of the service which is provided. The change in question has been the movement away from long-stay residential institutions. The policy was initially developed in the early 1960s, when 'community care' was mainly thought of as an issue in mental health[9] – slightly perversely, because many of those who were discharged as a consequence were people with learning disabilities, some with severe physical disabilities, who often lived in the same institutions as people with mental health problems. In England, much of the process of discharge from institutions had been completed by the late 1980s; in Scotland, it took at least twenty years longer, and while there are still residential institutions in both countries, they are nothing like as prevalent as they were. Long-stay care for geriatric patients shifted substantially in the 1980s and 1990s, and the private sector (heavily subsidised at that time by the social security system) grew at extraordinary speed. The reforms of social care after 1990 shifted the responsibility for care to local authorities, but many of the changes had taken place before that. The discussion of much of this trend has become part of the discussion of social care, which is discussed in Chapter 4, rather than health care. But the distinction between health and social care conceals one of the central differences between the NHS in the 1940s and 1950s and the NHS now. The NHS used to be a provider for all the needs of people

---

[6] For example, A Pollock, 2004, *NHS plc*, London: Verso; J Davis, J Lister, D Wrigley, 2015, *NHS for sale*, London: Merlin.

[7] M Powell, 2019, The English National Health Service in a cold climate, in E Heins, J Rees, C Needham (eds) *Social policy review 31*, Bristol: Policy Press.

[8] Department of Health and Social Care, 2021, *Integration and innovation: working together to improve health and social care for all*, https://assets.publishing.service.gov.uk/government/uploads/system/uploads/attachment_data/file/960548/integration-and-innovation-working-together-to-improve-health-and-social-care-for-all-web-version.pdf

[9] A Scull, 1977, *Decarceration*, Englewood Cliffs: Prentice Hall.

with severe disabilities – food, accommodation, warmth, lifestyle and social contact. It did those things rather badly, because the model of a hospital did not fit the needs, but that criticism is no longer particularly relevant; the NHS has moved on. It has focussed instead on a central role, which is to provide medical care.

What the NHS does

The Constitution of the NHS – or at least, of the Constitution of the NHS in England – describes what it does in these terms:

> The NHS belongs to the people. It is there to improve our health and well-being, supporting us to keep mentally and physically well, to get better when we are ill and, when we cannot fully recover, to stay as well as we can to the end of our lives. It works at the limits of science – bringing the highest levels of human knowledge and skill to save lives and improve health. It touches our lives at times of basic human need, when care and compassion are what matter most.[10]

This is followed by seven core principles:

1. The NHS provides a comprehensive service, available to all.
2. Access to NHS services is based on clinical need, not an individual's ability to pay.
3. The NHS aspires to the highest standards of excellence and professionalism.
4. The patient will be at the heart of everything the NHS does.
5. The NHS works across organisational boundaries and in partnership with other organisations in the interest of patients, local communities and the wider population.
6. The NHS is committed to providing best value for taxpayers' money and the most effective, fair and sustainable use of finite resources.
7. The NHS is accountable to the public, communities and patients that it serves.[11]

This all takes a great deal for granted. It does not say directly that the NHS is there to provide medical care, or even that people will be treated for illnesses. It does not say that people will be registered with a medical practice

---

[10] NHS, 2015, *The NHS Constitution: the NHS belongs to us all*, https://www.gov.uk/government/publications/the-nhs-constitution-for-england/the-nhs-constitution-for-england

[11] NHS, 2015.

responsible for their care. It does not say how clinical need is established – primarily by medical assessment and referral rather than personal demand. It does not say anything either about the limits of what the NHS will provide, or what has to be paid for – the painfully high charges for dentistry, for example, sit rather uncomfortably with core principle number 2.

The NHS may contribute to improving health and well-being, but neither of those terms helps much to explain what it does. There are important services in the UK that used to be thought of as 'health' – public housing, sanitation and food quality among them. Those are all now treated as something rather different. If we consider some of the issues that are currently prominent in shaping the health of the population – such as diet, smoking, pollution and poverty – we find that, although health professionals certainly have a lot to say on the issues, neither medical care in general, nor the health service in particular, has necessarily been the locus of the response.

What the NHS mainly does in practice is to cover many (but not all) of the needs which arise related to medical care. The areas covered include primary care, acute care in hospitals, some ancillary services and some medical goods (nearly all in hospital, only some in ambulant care). The rights that the health service guarantees are rights to medical care, not to specific treatments: people should be assessed medically and offered treatments that are considered appropriate by a qualified professional.

The care that people receive is, for the most part, defined on medical criteria, or 'clinical need'. In recent years the NHS has qualified that commitment by gradually restricting the delivery of services to those which are proven to be clinically effective and offering some degree of value for money. For most of the time since 1948, doctors were able to identify whatever treatment they thought fit – it was a matter of the clinical freedom of the doctor. That meant that it was possible, for example, for patients to receive homeopathic treatments, paid for by the NHS, if their doctor thought it appropriate. That level of freedom has gradually been reduced – for example it became possible in hospitals, and then in pharmacies more generally, for pharmacists to substitute generic drugs in place of those that were specifically recommended; and after that the NHS started to restrict the range of pharmaceuticals it was ready to pay for, such as for pain relief. The introduction of NICE, originally the 'National Institute for Clinical Excellence' and now the 'National Institute for Health and Care Excellence', has led to a much greater uniformity in the standards and quality of treatments that are available. NICE is often treated in the press as a cost-cutting exercise, because of its role in limiting the use of expensive treatments with relatively little marginal benefit. That is unfair; the reports are much more concerned with scientific evidence, much more open to a range of views, and more closely reasoned, than this suggests. What the reports look for, generally in consultation with scientists, clinical specialists and representatives of patients, is evidence that a treatment is effective, what benefits it offers, and how it compares to other available treatments. One of the key tools for comparison is the QALY or quality-adjusted life year. The test is not simply a test of cost, but of value for money: how much it costs for people to have a good quality of life, and more of it.[12] There are special rules, and more liberal standards, governing end-of-life care.

The implication of any rationing procedure in the NHS is that the services offered will not be really comprehensive. Rationing is sometimes seen as a new development, but it has been done throughout the life of the NHS.[13] There are circumstances in which people will have a wide range of needs met as part of the service – for example, receiving free food while in hospital – and others where the range of support seems hugely limited, for example in assistance while recuperating at home. They are, however, largely universal, in the sense of being available for the whole population. The main problem with making services accessible to everyone that is that access to health services depends on registration with a general practitioner (GP). There are areas of the country, particularly London, where large numbers of people are not registered, or need to report for care in an area where they do not actually live. (The official counts are surprisingly vague. Apparently there are more people registered with GPs than there are in the total population, but there are no figures for how many people are not registered.[14]) There are areas of the country where it is difficult to find an open list – one of the contributing factors to heavy over-use of hospitals for minor ailments. Homeless people in particular have difficulty gaining access to primary care, because without an address it is generally impossible to register.

Equally, only part of the service is free at the point of delivery. Consultations with GPs and referrals to hospitals are made without charge. There are mixed approaches: assistance with travel to hospitals in an ambulance is usually free (for road traffic accidents, there is some cross-charging to car insurance), but meeting the costs of travel to hospitals for outpatient appointments has usually been residual and means-tested. Several services ancillary to medicine, including optics, dentistry and pharmacy, have complex rules, which are different in different parts of the UK. Charges were first introduced in 1950. There have been repeated arguments, almost since the inception of the NHS, to introduce more charges. (The high costs

---

[12] C Phillips, G Thomson, 2001, *What is a QALY?*, http://www.bandolier.org.uk/painres/download/whatis%20copy/QALY.pdf

[13] See, for example, T Halper, 1985, Life and death in a welfare state: end stage renal disease in the United Kingdom, *Milbank Memorial Fund Quarterly*, 63(1), pp 52–93.

[14] H Gye, 2020, Fears for future of Covid vaccine roll-out as Government doesn't know how many people aren't signed up to a GP, *i newspaper*, 16 December, https://inews.co.uk/news/politics/fears-future-covid-vaccine-roll-out-gp-latest-news-798128

of medical care, and an extensive system of exemptions, imply that charges make very little contribution to costs.) Several services are subject to charges: they include dentistry, optics and (in England) community pharmacy. An Act of 1988 removed free eye tests in England. Many prescriptions are still issued free – mainly to old people and children; as charges have risen fewer people pay the formal charge, because they get cheaper drugs privately. In Scotland, eye tests and prescriptions have been again made free.

This all invites a different interpretation of what the NHS is actually doing. It is not providing or securing people's 'health' – medical care is not at all the same thing. It does not offer medical care on demand. It is not comprehensive, and it is not unlimited. A report on NHS performance comments:

> The NHS has definite strengths relative to other health systems. It provides unusually good financial protection to the public from the consequences of ill health; it appears to be relatively efficient; and it performs well in managing some long-term conditions. It does all this with an unusually low level of staffing and, in at least some categories, equipment. However, the NHS does not have especially good outcomes relative to other wealthy countries. For the most important illnesses in directly causing death, it is a consistently below-average performer.[15]

One of the chief benefits provided by the NHS is largely invisible. The 'universal' element in the NHS does not lie in the way that individuals are treated, because that is based on professional judgments about need. It is universal because everyone is covered, receiving (whether they use it or not) the equivalent of medical insurance, which in other countries they would have to pay for. Like an insurance policy, there are terms and conditions governing what will be paid for and when; but it is an insurance that does not require specific or individualised contributions.

Preventative health care

Preventative health care has not been one of the major focuses of the NHS, but it is hardly possible, writing this book in the middle of a pandemic, to pass over it. There are two main types of prevention. Primary prevention aims to stop people from developing a problem in the first place. This might be done by changing the environment. The public health measures of the mid-nineteenth century focussed on sewers, water supplies and food adulteration; in the early twentieth century the focus moved to housing

---

[15] M Dayan, D Ward, T Gardiner, E Kelly, 2018, *How good is the NHS?*, London: Health Foundation, Institute for Fiscal Studies, King's Fund and Nuffield Trust.

and nutrition. It might be done by changing people's behaviour. This is attempted through health education; advertising; legal restrictions, like licensing of pubs; and financial disincentives, like taxation on cigarettes and alcohol. And it might be done by changing people's condition: vaccination is the obvious example. Secondary prevention is based on identifying a problem in its early stages to prevent its progression, for example through screening of women for breast and cervical cancer, or enabling women to have an abortion after amniocentesis identifying that a child may be disabled.

The NHS's commitment to improving the health of the population was for a long time interpreted purely in terms of medical care. Prevention received a low priority, and tended to be confined to such issues as vaccination, school health and post-natal care. The importance of cost brought prevention to attention in the 1970s, although it is still only a very limited part of the NHS budget. Prominent issues in preventive medicine have included, for example, smoking, poor diet and obesity, and alcohol. Smoking has the largest effect. The major fatal diseases in Britain − cancer, stroke and heart disease − are clearly and directly related to it. Smoking is also an evident cause of major impairment, including respiratory ailments and circulatory diseases. The government's response has been to combine health education with financial disincentives in the form of high taxation. This has been surprisingly effective; more than eight million adults in Britain have given up since the campaigns started. By contrast, relatively little progress has been made into poor diet and obesity, which are two of the top five factors leading to premature death − but the NHS has disturbingly little input into either, bar 'advice' about a healthy diet. Alcohol, too, remains a major problem. The NHS records that more than 1.2 million admissions to hospital in England are either attributable directly to alcohol, or have problems with alcohol as a secondary diagnosis.[16] This accounts for 7.2% of all hospital admissions, but 15% or more of Accident and Emergency (A and E) admissions. The emphasis has fallen on changing behaviour. The most positive effects have been in circumstances where the propaganda is linked to other measures, such as the impact of the breathalyser on drunken driving; but propaganda alone has little apparent effect. It is early days, and the pattern has been interrupted by the pandemic, but minimum pricing of alcohol in Scotland, introduced in 2018, seems to have had a positive effect in reducing consumption.[17] Apart from that, the most promising preventative measures for the near future, apart from those associated with the pandemic,

[16] NHS, 2019, *Statistics on alcohol, England 2019*, https://digital.nhs.uk/data-and-information/publications/statistical/statistics-on-alcohol/2019/part-1

[17] A O'Donnell, P Anderson, E Jane-Lopis, J Manthey, E Kaner, J Rehm, 2019, Immediate impact of minimum unit pricing on alcohol purchases in Scotland, *British Medical Journal*, 366(8215), https://www.bmj.com/content/366/bmj.l5274

fall outwith the scope of medical care: increasing income, and restricting the adulteration of foods with sugar.

Medical care is heavily individualised: ill-health is taken patient by patient. That has affected the way that health promotion services operate, although they work to principles that can be generalised across broad categories of patient, and it has influenced the way that prevention is currently understood. The main responses to issues of diet or alcohol abuse, for example, have been to encourage individuals to change their behaviour, despite abundant evidence that the most effective interventions have been general and aimed at populations. Education about the risks of smoking has been far less effective than two relatively indiscriminate interventions: increasing the taxes on tobacco, and banning smoking in public places. The arguments for minimum pricing of alcohol, or sugar taxes, fall into similar categories; 'libertarians' see these things as a matter of individual choice. Similarly, the objections to many of the measures taken to curb the pandemic – restrictions on travel, wearing face masks or meeting in groups – are individualised, while the justifications for these policies have been collective. There is a continuing tension between public and individual priorities, seen, for example, in resistance to vaccines, such as the triple vaccine given to children, and most powerfully in the course of the pandemic.

For most of the last fifty years – at least, since 1974, when preventative services were brought out of local government, and unified with the health service – this has all been classified as public health, understood as 'health promotion'. The coronavirus pandemic has called us back to the 'public health' of a different era: a set of measures that have been concerned, not so much with prevention and education, but in population-based measures intended to control the spread of, and harm done by, a deadly disease. And one of the immediate implications for policy was that Public Health England, a body set up with the general remit of health promotion and education, was not necessarily geared to managing the very different tasks of infection control, testing and contact tracing, for which the primary expertise was to be found in health care trusts.

The idea of 'public health' still makes sense, but is based in arguments that are not addressed by conventional medical care, and not focused on individuals. First, public health is justified in terms of the interests of broader populations. Individuals may benefit because they are also part of a wider society, but the test is not whether any single person is personally better off. Ill health can have externalities. If people are given a 'choice' to carry untreated infections, the harm that is done is harm to other people – a point that seemed to get lost among those defending the right of care workers not to be vaccinated. And an individual's exposure to risk is inadequate as a basis for protecting the health of a wider population. An individual may reasonably accept a chance of one in a thousand against dying from a disease

– the risk may reasonably seem remote – but in a country of 67 million people, that implies that 67,000 people will die. That was more or less the calculation six months into the pandemic. At the time of writing, that round figure is close to half the actual death rate. If decisions about risk are left to individual judgment, the collective consequences can be devastating.

Distractions

Individualisation is only one of the persistent themes that recur in discussions of health services. The Darzi report on health services rehearses many of the common tropes: more preventative measures, more 'joined up' services, greater accessibility, more personalised services, and (of course) further reorganisation at the centre.[18] Martin Powell comments that there is a sense of a 'Groundhog Day'[19]: the same arguments come up repeatedly on the merry-go-round, never achieving the results that they promise. Most of the themes in that list are concerned with issues beyond the health service, and I will return to them in due course.

The greatest distraction, however, has been of a different order: it is the recurring belief that what the NHS needs is the discipline of commercial markets, and that market-based solutions would offer citizens more choice, more control and better access. The NHS has always had some elements of private practice,[20] but the tone changed with the insistence, in the 1980s, that the NHS should be run more like a business. Many of the administrative reforms taking place since the 1980s have been founded in the fervent belief that private enterprise does things better, and if the NHS can be run more like a business, it will be better too. There are three main confusions in that. One is a misunderstanding of how business works. Businesses are supposed (in theory, at least) to be in competition, and have an incentive to be 'efficient', meaning that they are able to produce the maximum number of units of output for the minimum cost. The way a market works does not depend only on the choices of consumers: business make choices, too, about what they do and how they do it. They determine what can be done profitably and efficiently, what can not, and leave the things they cannot do to their competitors. Private enterprise always leaves gaps; that is what is supposed to happen. (The same kinds of consideration are commonly found when businesses contract to deliver a service. Hodge comments that 'some suppliers have lost sight of the fact that they are delivering public services, and that brings with it an

---

[18] Lord Darzi (Chair), 2018, *Better health and care for all*, London: Institute for Public Policy Research.

[19] Powell, 2019.

[20] M Powell, R Miller, 2016, Seventy years of privatising the British National Health Service, *Social Policy and Administration*, 50(1), pp 99–118.

expectation to do so in accordance with public services standards.'[21] That should not be surprising. When they perform well, businesses do what they are signed up to do; they do not go above and beyond that.)

The second problem with relying on the market concerns the management of risk. Businesses take risks, including the risk of not being able to complete a task. If they fail in a commercial market, they go out of business. The NHS does not have the option of going out of business. Nursing care for elderly people cannot be discontinued because an operator is bankrupt. That makes nonsense of a competitive model that relies on free entry to and exit from the market. Effectively the NHS has to act as a guarantor of essential work. As one witness told the inquiry into a failing hospital:

> [*Witness*] These contracts, okay, you can argue they're legally binding, but the reality is that how do you implement a contract when you've got a service like [this] hospital …? The ultimate sanction is you either close the hospital or you take significant funds away. Neither is an option …
>
> [*The Chairman*]: Does it amount, then, to an acceptance that to some extent, not completely, the concept of commissioning by contract is a little bit of a fiction?
>
> [*Witness*]: My own personal view that in these circumstances … the contract could be described as a fiction, because if it has no teeth, how do you implement the penalty that drives the contract?[22]

What happens effectively is that the state, implicitly or explicitly, accepts the consequences of such activities when they are undertaken within the public sector, and underwrites public services activities when they are commissioned from the private sector. That raises a strong case, even where activities might be done more cheaply elsewhere, for maintaining them in the public sector.

The third problem is the supposition that the skills for running health care are the same as those for running a business. No special knowledge or expertise is required, beyond 'leadership', loosely identified as the ability to run an organisation. Appointments made during the pandemic to head up Public Health England and Track and Trace have been made on this basis. The idea of 'leadership' is used all too often to wave aside requirements for competence.[23]

---

[21] Cited in J Davis et al, 2015, p 176.

[22] R Francis (Chair), 2013, *Report of the Mid Staffordshire NHS Foundation Trust Public Inquiry*, vol 1, 7.338, HC 898-1, London: TSO.

[23] P Spicker, 2012, 'Leadership': a perniciously vague concept, *International Journal of Public Sector Management*, 25(1), pp 34–47.

The delivery of medical care

Some of the problems faced by the NHS are the problems of any health care system in the developed world: for example, an ageing population, ailments produced by contemporary lifestyles, such as drug dependency, obesity or diabetes, the deficiencies of psychiatric medicine, or the management of the pandemic. Some of the problems relate to the particular history and development of the NHS: the uneven distribution of resources relative to the population (such as the concentration of hospitals in inner London), the perverse incentives that consultants in some fields may still have to extend their waiting lists, or the rather eccentric relationship to private medicine which makes it possible for private patients to gain accelerated entry to NHS health facilities. Some problems represent the negative consequences of attempts to respond to those issues: the influence of targets, the process of 'gaming' to look good on performance indicators while making services worse (such as holding people in ambulances in the car park outside the hospital), and (as the Francis Report records)[24] the loss of focus on patient care while all eyes are set on management criteria. There are continuing problems, too, of staff shortages, with a general shortfall of recruitment and training leaving something in the region of 30% of posts unfilled, and particular problems in areas that might be more isolated, less salubrious or less able to offer a promising career path. This is only a short chapter, and it is not going to be possible to cover everything.

Some of the big issues requiring reform, however, are fundamental to the delivery of medical care. They concern the balance between primary care, on one hand, and acute care in hospitals (and especially emergency care) on the other. The division in British medicine, which predates the NHS, developed on the principle that general practitioners would receive and identify initial problems, and refer cases to secondary care in hospital as necessary.[25] There has been some departure from that principle, in both directions: GPs have come increasingly to conduct continuing care for complex, long-term health issues, and hospitals are more likely to receive problems at first instance. The NHS website tells us that GPs deal with more than 300 million consultations every year; A and E units deal with 23 million.[26] A little over 41 million consultations were held in outpatient departments.[27] The 2019 NHS Plan puts the total number of consultations

[24] Francis, 2013.

[25] F Honigsbaum, 1981, *The division in British medicine 1911–1968*, London: Kogan Page.

[26] NHS, 2017, *NHS five year forward view*, https://www.england.nhs.uk/five-year-forward-view/next-steps-on-the-nhs-five-year-forward-view/primary-care/

[27] R Jones, P White, D Armstrong, M Ashworth, M Peters, 2010, *Managing acute illness*, London: King's Fund.

at the higher figure of 400 million.[28] Taken together, it is likely that more than 80% of all ambulant illness and continuing care is being dealt with by GPs. The British Medical Association has been arguing that general practice is in serious difficulties, in recruitment, finance, staffing and equipment: half all the practices in England would like to close their list to new patients. 'The foundation on which the NHS sits today is cracking and can no longer withstand the weight it is expected to bear.'[29]

Despite the importance of primary care, the NHS has been dominated throughout its life by hospital care. That is reflected in the distribution of resources, statuses within the medical profession, and the pre-eminence in particular of university hospitals. Arguably it also reflects the pattern of professional training. Doctors are encouraged to think of themselves as scientists, and hospital medicine is the height of real science. Hospital medicine works primarily with identifiable conditions where the object is to respond to those conditions with the best scientific response, and wherever possible to advance the science of the discipline. General practice, by contrast, deals primarily with uncertainty and the human condition, aiming to manage and narrow the scope of that uncertainty. If hospital medicine is science, general practice is art (and no less challenging for that).

The quality of general practice in the NHS has improved immeasurably from its early days: specialist training, improved financial arrangements and group practice have meant that practices have more resources and GPs have the backup of a team. (The numbers of single-handed practitioners halved after 2000.) The Care Quality Commission (CQC) rates 89% of general practices in England as good, and 5% as outstanding.[30] From the point of view of patients, however, there are some visible deficiencies. Because GPs are both the gatekeepers of the system and the managers of continuing care, issues of access and continuity are critical. Successive reforms have meant that getting to see a GP has become more difficult, and getting to see a named GP more difficult still. In the 1950s, people had a right to be registered with a doctor, and a right to be medically examined; that used to mean that the doctor had a duty to visit. After the 'doctors' charter' in the 1960s, it became routine for GPs to hire relief doctors to cover out-of-hours services. The coverage for medical examination out of hours became intermittent, and in further reforms the duty was effectively passed to an alternative service, NHS 24. The 'right to be seen' for many people became a trip to hospital, not uncommonly via the A and E department. That trend has been compounded by changes in lifestyle: people are far less likely to

---

[28] NHS, 2019, *The NHS long term plan*, London: NHS, p 6.

[29] British Medical Association, 2017, *Saving general practice*, London: BMA, p 3.

[30] Care Quality Commission (CQC), 2020, *The state of health care and adult social care in England 2019/20*, London: House of Commons, HC 799, pp 16–17.

work in the same place where they live or are registered with a GP, and some of them will have to look for services on the spot. The number of people present in London during the normal working week, pre-pandemic, was about four million more than live there. The NHS Long Term Plan, issued before the pandemic, foresaw a substantial shift away from face to face consultations, towards 'digitally enabled' communication.[31] It is difficult to say as yet how far this is truly 'digital' as opposed to consultation by telephone; remote advice giving has greatly expanded.

Although A and E is rather less important as a deliverer of primary care than GPs are, the growth of A and E has had a major impact in its own right. The argument for A and E was fundamentally an argument for centralisation, particularly in areas where university hospitals were dominant. 'Casualty' was fused with major trauma services, on the basis that any casualty might prove to be major. However, these services also became the receiving points for relatively minor ailments. The effect of winter flu or norovirus has been to squeeze hospitals in three ways – making it difficult both to manage the number of demands of treatment, impairing the ability of hospitals to function as staff are affected, and making it difficult to move patients on to appropriate care. By contrast with general practice, the CQC rates half of urgent and emergency care services in England as being in need of improvement or inadequate.[32] The primary duty of any hospital is to do no harm, and one has to ask whether it can ever have been the best approach to take every presenting problem and to channel it through a particular route during an epidemic.

The original argument for A and E was that every hospital should be capable of dealing with the problems that might be presented. The same kind of argument, that every hospital should have the capacity to deal with situations comprehensively, was being made throughout the health service, taking in such services as maternity or heart surgery. The deficiencies of that approach are now better understood. It is not practical to maintain comprehensive services everywhere, because it calls for specialist teams, equipment, training and the opportunity to develop expertise. It implies either that units which are ill-equipped for the task will attempt to do things they do not have enough experience to do – the source of major problems, for example, in heart surgery and paediatrics – or that routine tasks will be centralised along with the specialised ones (which is, more or less, what has happened with A and E).

At the very least, this calls for a recalibration of service priorities. The Darzi report wanted services to be based around a 'neighbourhood NHS', which might sound good to people in metropolitan areas but would not offer

---

[31] NHS, 2019.
[32] CQC, 2020, p 17.

a feasible pattern for much of the country.[33] The Kerr report in Scotland was much more sensitive to locational issues.[34] The Kerr committee undertook an exemplary consultative process, listening to a wide range of views, and giving particular attention to the problems of remote and rural areas. They proposed a layered structure, reflecting the complexity and degree of specialisation required. In particular, they recommended the breakup of A and E into its constituent parts. Kerr graded those by seriousness, but I think might be better understood if it is seen as a distinction between 'casualty' and 'trauma'. This all makes eminently good sense, but good sense is no guarantee of political feasibility. Its implementation led almost immediately to protests in Ayr and Monklands, where a proposal to decentralise, replacing two A and E units with four casualty units and one trauma centre, led to public protests, and a new government took the popular step of stopping the change (though not in others). Despite the setback, Kerr's approach has proved itself. Its impact can be seen in the growth of community hospitals, which provide general practice services along with a range of professions ancillary to medicine, including, for example, radiography, nursing, podiatry, pharmacy, physiotherapy and outpatient consultancies.

The same principles guide the reform of hospital care and primary care. The central objective has to be to provide a service that is universal and comprehensive. To do that, the response has to be structured. It does not follow, because a service is comprehensive, that every specialism should be available at every level. If people could be dealt with wholly at the point of contact, there would be no point in having more remote services; if every front-line professional had the same competence, there would be no need for specialists. A structured response, and a division of labour, is the most effective way to offer expert services when they are needed.

---

[33] Darzi, 2018, ch 5.

[34] D Kerr, 2005, *A report on the future of the NHS in Scotland*, Edinburgh: Scottish Government, http://www.scotland.gov.uk/Publications/2005/05/23141307/13135

The National Health Service

Key points	The NHS offers a form of insurance, providing medical care to anyone.
	Despite the dominance of hospitals, general practice is at the heart of what the NHS does.
	The need for public health has been highlighted by recent experience.
Positive developments	The NHS has moved away from long-stay institutions and focused on medical care.
	General practice has been greatly improved.
Where policy has gone wrong	Private markets cannot fill the gaps. They depend on producers having choices, and that leads to exclusion.
	Health is public as well as individual. Reducing everything to the personal level compromises the aims of health services.
What to do instead	The health service has to provide different levels of service: decentralised general services, more specialised work for larger areas, and highly specialised centralised provision.

4

Social care

By contrast with the health service, social care has a much more residual focus, coupled with an individualist emphasis on independence, personal choice and commercialised services. The idea of 'social care', as we now understand the term, was hardly thought of at the time when the NHS was founded; 'community care' emerged as an issue in the 1960s, and social care has emerged as a major theme largely because of changes in other services. At the time of the welfare state's foundation, the main provision for frail older people or people with severe disabilities would have implied either long-stay hospital provision or residential care under Part III of the National Assistance Act, mainly provided by local authority Welfare Departments. The 'personal social services' – provision by Welfare, Health and Children's Departments – had only limited involvement with care in people's own homes, and in the case of Health and Welfare, that involvement was mainly linked to hospitals or day care. In the early 1960s there was an extension of two main types of domiciliary support, meals on wheels and home helps; depending on the area, there may also have been some day care provision. Home helps were provided through the Health Departments; meals on wheels and residential care were the responsibility of the Welfare Department. Occupational therapists worked in either service.

The new Social Services Departments (or Social Work Departments, in Scotland), formed from the three existing departments, were supposed to deliver adult social care, but this consistently received less attention and a lower priority than children's services. During the 1980s, central government opted to develop in particular the residential care sector, with a strong emphasis on private provision; the costs were paid as part of Supplementary Benefit. The result was a rapid expansion of private residential and nursing care, which went in about ten years from being on the margins of provision to equal the local authority sector in size.

The Griffiths report of 1988[1] proposed a rationalisation of a sort: that local authorities should be in charge of the service, that the money being provided by the social security system should go through local authorities instead, and that services should be provided by multiple providers and paid for by multiple purchasers. That has been the policy ever since; the current fashion for personalisation and individual budgets is a reiteration of the Griffiths principles in another guise. There has been a progressive transfer

---

[1] R Griffiths, 1988, *Community care: agenda for action*, London: HMSO.

of services into the private sector; private firms supply three-quarters of staff for residential and home care, and the private sector is increasingly the province of larger providers, providing services 'that minimise the number of staff needed and maximise cash generation, rather than reflecting the needs of service users'.[2] The largest five firms provide almost 20% of all beds in care homes, but there are many actors in the field. In care homes, some 5,500 providers provide for 410,000 residents; in home care, more than 10,000 providers deliver support to 900,000 people.[3] There are recurring problems of quality, workforce planning and finance.[4] The COVID-19 crisis has exposed a further weakness: that people who live in close proximity to each other are more vulnerable to infection, and the risks are greatly magnified in larger care homes. The death rates have been disturbingly high.[5]

The Griffiths reforms also had an important institutional effect; they greatly expanded the role of Social Services Departments in the provision of adult care. As both social care and child protection have expanded, many local authorities have separated out adult social care from children's services.

Residential care

There are lots of strands to disentangle here, and the only practical way to go about it is to take them one by one. The first part of the picture may not seem to be about 'social care' at all; it is about residential care. Most residential care is in 'care homes' or 'nursing homes', but there is a wide range of residential services. The Wagner report identified nine main categories:

- *Long-term care.* This is the most commonly recognised pattern, including many old people's homes, children's homes, and so on.
- *Respite care*, to give carers a break.
- *Assessment.* A number of homes – particularly for children – are designed as temporary stages, during which a person's needs can be assessed and a suitable placement found.
- *Rehabilitation.* Some homes – like probation hostels or hostels for former psychiatric patients – are concerned with enabling someone to return to the community.

---

[2] B Hudson, 2016, *The failure of privatised adult social care in England*, Centre for Health and the Public Interest, p 8, www.chpi.org.uk

[3] B Hudson, 2019, Commissioning for change, *Critical Social Policy*, 39(3), pp 413–33.

[4] Care Quality Commission (CQC), 2020, *The state of health care and adult social care in England 2019/20*, London: House of Commons, HC 799.

[5] CQC, 2020, p 35.

- *Therapy or treatment.* Examples are hostels for people with drug dependencies, and some hostels for mentally ill people.
- *Training.* There are homes and hostels of this type, for example, for mentally handicapped people or mothers with young children.
- *Convalescence,* for example, nursing homes for the elderly or for some psychiatric patients.
- *Crisis or emergencies.*
- *Shared care or flexible care* – arrangements which are increasingly being made for elderly or physically disabled people.[6]

The arguments for having some kinds of residential care are strong. Care homes make it possible to provide services intensively for people with high dependency – going well beyond monitoring their situation, cleaning or providing meals, because that can be done in ordinary housing. Providing intensive services to people in independent, separate homes would require far more by way of trained staff, resources and organisational management. But the same intensive provision would be inappropriate for many people – many private care homes offering long-term care are occupied in part by people who do not really need a high level of service, but who enter residential care regardless.

Long-stay hospitals have gradually been closed down, and have almost disappeared; when older people are admitted to hospital, the primary objective is to restore them to a state where they can be moved on. When people come into hospital for acute care, it might not be possible to discharge them back to their home. When that happens, there are two main outcomes, neither of which is desirable: either they can stay in hospital, 'blocking' beds and losing capacity, or they can be discharged to something that isn't necessarily appropriate to their needs, typically a care home that happens to be available. The division of labour between health and social care has become, Daly comments, deeply institutionalised; and the lack of co-ordination and oversight between the services certainly played a role in the horrifying death rate in care homes in the early stages of the pandemic.[7]

The central reason for the growth of residential care, as for much of the development of community care, was not based in the positive strengths of residential services: it was a reaction against the long-stay hospitals. Old people in need of care were often forced to live in places which were incapable of providing them with a decent living environment. Long-stay care conjured a picture of large Poor Law institutions. The worst examples were often given by long-stay hospital care, which offered a grossly inappropriate

---

[6] G Wagner (Chair), 1988, *Residential care: a positive choice*, London: HMSO, p 166.

[7] M Daly, 2020, Covid-19 and care homes in England, *Social Policy and Administration*, 54(7), pp 985–98.

model for residential living; the 'Nightingale' ward, a dormitory laid out so that one nurse can see instantly when something is wrong, was excellent for acute care but hardly created the sort of environment you would want to live in. Too often there were bad physical conditions, low standards of care, and a disturbing catalogue of scandals showing the neglect and ill-treatment of residents. But residential homes did not offer much better. Some residential care was 'warehousing', simply somewhere to put the people. A common image was of 'very old people dozing or staring into space in identical chairs placed around the walls of a large lounge, lining up for toileting and bathing, being dressed by hurried night staff early in the morning and then waiting more than an hour for breakfast'.[8] Residential care was treated as a last resort, desirable only for those who were unable to cope in the community. That impression was reinforced whenever some of the scandals that had blighted long-stay institutions[9] – problems of maltreatment of vulnerable people who had been isolated from society – were reflected in the residential care sector.

When it came to expanding the provision of residential care in the 1980s, the government opted to do it through the private sector. Part of the case for doing it that way was certainly ideological – the private sector, the government of the time believed, simply did things better. Part was practical; the private sector was able to develop services at a much faster rate than the public services ever could, partly because they could draw on finance that state-based services couldn't, and perhaps because they did not have so many hoops to jump through. That part of the design worked; the sector developed at breath-taking speed. It is easy to imagine that residential and nursing care have always been there. In fact, most of the private sector is less than forty years old, conjured into existence by the imaginative use of social security and subsequently redefined as 'community care'. The main weakness was that the finances were dependent on two sources: the services commissioned by public authorities, which were always done under constraint, and the private resources of the residents, which could be exhausted if the resident lived too long.

Much of the attention that has been devoted to 'social care' in past years has actually been about the cost of residential care. The NHS provides services generically, according to need, and does not charge for its services. The social care system is primarily based on individualised, and often on market-based, services; people's ability to command a service depends on either on the resources they can command, or on means-testing. Several

---

[8] E M Goldberg, N Connolly, 1983, *The effectiveness of social care for the elderly*, London: Heinemann.

[9] J Martin, 1985, *Hospitals in trouble*, Oxford: Blackwell.

sources attribute the disparity to the 1948 settlement,[10] but much of it is the product of subsequent developments: the arrangements that were made in the 1960s as long-stay hospitals started to close, the expansion in the 1960s of local authority 'welfare' services covering domiciliary care, and the expansion of residential care in the 1980s. The cost of residential care can be expected to force people coming into care to sell their houses, and in some cases it can swallow all the capital value. This is the situation that the Dilnot Commission was addressed to,[11] as was the ill-starred Conservative Party manifesto of 2015, which promised that no one would have to sell their home to pay for care; the most recent proposals offer less, but focus on the same issues.[12] Unfortunately, the leading providers of residential care use a viper's nest of financial mechanisms that are designed to extract and siphon off resources from the system in a way that is inherently unstable. Debt-laden 'operational' companies, which actually deliver the service, pay 'rent' to invented property companies, unnecessarily high interest to finance companies, and management charges to other companies in the group. All are generally controlled by the same people. Burns and her colleagues comment: 'Putting more money in to the system via higher weekly payments per bed will not produce a robust and sustainable care home sector when the financialised providers are so adept at taking money out.'[13]

It may have seemed plausible to argue that a competitive private sector would be more responsive than public authorities responsive to purchasers and service users, but elderly residents are vulnerable and constrained in their choices, and local authority care managers have found they could not rely on cash and contracts alone to protect residents' interests. The CQC has expressed concern that 'the continuing lack of a long-term sustainable solution for adult social care was having a damaging impact on the quality and quantity of available care'.[14] Care homes, they report, are relying on their self-financing residents to keep going; homes which have more than three-quarters of their residents paid for by local authorities are in trouble. Hudson points to a dangerous combination of a low-skilled, underpaid

---

[10] For example, K Barker (Chair), 2014, *A new settlement for health and social care*, London: King's Fund; C Smith, 2018, *NHS and integrated health care services*, House of Lords Library Briefing; House of Commons Health and Social Care Committee, 2018, *Integrated care*, HC 650.

[11] Commission on Funding of Care and Support, 2011, *Fairer care funding*, https://tinyurl.com/yy85jbr

[12] Conservative Party, 2015, *The Conservative Party manifesto 2015*, p 65.

[13] D Burns, L Cowie, J Earle, P Folkman, J Froud, P Hyde, S Johal, I Rees Jones, A Killett, K Williams, 2016, *Where does the money go?*, Manchester: CRESC (Centre for Research on Socio-Cultural Change), p 25.

[14] CQC, 2020, p 23.

workforce, unsound financial models, and a strong risk of market failure as debt-laden providers crash out of the market.[15]

Finance is not the only issue, by any means; it matters no less what people are being asked to spend so much money to get. Residential care is not an ideal way to meet needs. Some problems are inherent in the provision of residential care. A care home is not the same as a person's own home, in an important respect. All residential care has an element of group living – cleaning, TV rooms, common areas for meals and so forth. The Wagner report argued that this should be seen as a combination of accommodation plus support, where people made a positive choice for group living, but the level of support that was available should be adapted flexibly to the needs of the person.[16] That approach was always unrealistic; it failed to engage with the things that residential care actually does. Support and accommodation are planned and delivered together because it is much more practical (and less expensive) to arrange support and specialised items in a specific location. There are good organisational reasons why residential units should offer a specific pattern of services, in terms of administration, competence and control. Some residential care, such as care for older people, is fairly generic; some is highly specialised, with an identifiable programme of services. Residential care brings resources and expertise together in one place: it makes it possible to provide a wide range of specific types of service, delivered by specific kinds of staff.

As a general proposition, the move to group living requires people to change their life. There are many circumstances in which that level of change will not be appropriate – where there is a mismatch between the needs of the residents and the level of service which is being provided there. Wherever residential care is appropriate, the services it provides will be extensive, and it will be expensive; there is a clear case for social provision, pooling risks to pay for high levels of care. However, most care homes have come to depend on the presence of a proportion of more independent paying customers, who do not have the same need for intensive support. That makes the idea of long-term care insurance problematic, because the services in any residential unit, and so the costs that residents become liable for, are not easily related to any direct assessment of their personal needs. There is a case for the intensive resources to be made available for more broadly-based, flexible support networks – such as 'core and cluster' provision, where specialist staff and clients are located accessibly and near to each other, or 'very sheltered' housing, where accommodation is linked to optional high-dependency provision. There is a strong case, too, for 'lifelong' housing, which will be adaptable to increasing dependency. It might be

---

[15] Hudson, 2016.

[16] Wagner, 1988.

possible, on that basis, to reduce the role of residential care to some degree. However, we have to accept that residential care is there because there has to be an effective way of delivering services to people intensively. A care home may be the only practical option.

Staying in one's own home

The root of many of the problems of social care is a model that has been widely accepted for a very long time. The aim of maintaining old people in their own homes for as long as possible dates from Circular 2/62, on *Development of local authority health and welfare services*: 'Services for the elderly should be designed to help them remain in their own homes for as long as possible.'[17] We now have the experience of nearly sixty years of attempting to preserve independence in people's homes. In that time, the principle has rarely been challenged – the main exception has been the suggestion, from some feminists, that the effect of moving people out of institutions has been to transfer the burden of care, unpaid, to women.[18]

The principle of living in one's own home starts from a general proposition that I see no strong reason to disagree with – that people generally prefer to be in their own homes. There is not, admittedly, much evidence to back up the proposition, because there are not many circumstances in which people are actually given the free choice of being in their own home, or in someone else's, without the added dimension of insecurity in old age, incapacity or a radical loss of autonomy. Some of the people living in residential care have moved there although they have limited needs for support, and others have moved when they might have been able to receive more intensive support in their own homes. There are good reasons why people might want to stay where they currently live – identity, social networks, attachment to a particular location, satisfaction with their current accommodation – but people do still move housing at other points in their lives. There is no reason to suppose that people will not want to move simply because they are elderly, though it is probably true that people who have lived in a house for a longer period of time are more likely to find it satisfactory, because those who did not were more likely to have moved. Perhaps, if people had a meaningful choice between continuing to live in their own accommodation, or living in residential accommodation of their choice at the same price, more people would take the opportunity to move. Since most of us do not have those options, the issue is fairly academic.

---

[17] Circular 2/62, 1962, *Development of local authority Health and Welfare services*, London: HMSO.

[18] G Pascall, 1986, *Social policy: a feminist analysis*, London: Tavistock.

There are three key problems with the policy of maintaining independence in one's own home. The first rests in the weasel words, 'as long as possible'. How long is that? The question of what is possible depends on a range of issues – including, most obviously, the capacity of the elderly person, and the level of support available.

The second is the question of 'independence'. What is independence? If old people are receiving more and more support, are they still independent? And if 'independence' means that they sit neglected in one place because they are unable to move for long periods, is it worth having? Far too little emphasis is given to the principle that really matters – autonomy, or the ability to exercise control over one's own life. Autonomy depends on capacity, and capacity depends on the power to act.

The third problem is, to my mind, the most fundamental, because even if the first two are resolved, this one can never be. Built into the idea that people should be independent for as long as possible is the expectation that the time may come when it is not possible. We can extend the levels of support that are available. We can try to make people's lives more comfortable, and more bearable. But no matter how far the boundaries are pushed, there is liable to be a point where independence in one's own home is not possible. We have created a model where the decision to move people from their own homes is typically the result of a crisis – a tipping point where it is no longer possible for people to stay. The policy is catastrophic – that is not a metaphor. Either the policy kicks in when catastrophes happen, or short of that, it creates a catastrophe instead. Half the movement to residential care comes about because old people go into hospital, typically as the result of a fall or a medical emergency, and they cannot be discharged back to their own homes. Of those which come from people's own homes, there are a limited number of cases where old people choose to go into residential care while they are still relatively independent, but more typically they are placed there. Old people do not generally 'choose' to go to residential care; most are forced to it by circumstances. In about half of all cases, the decision is made for them, by family, carers or professionals.[19] Hudson refers to it as a 'distress purchase': people do not know what they are buying, or what the cost is, and they usually have to make the decision at a bad time.[20]

---

[19] I Allen, D Hogg, S Peace, 1992, *Elderly people: choice, participation and satisfaction*, London: Policy Studies Institute; S Davies, M Nolan, 2003 'Making the best of things': relatives' experience of decisions about care-home entry, *Ageing and Society*, 23, pp 429–50; H Arksey, C Glendinning, 2007, Choice in the context of informal care-giving, *Health and Social Care in the Community*, 15(2), pp 165–75.

[20] Hudson, 2016, p 12.

Domiciliary care: needs and assessment

The services that are provided for people in their own homes are supposed to meet their needs while not disrupting their lives. Some of these services are 'ambulant' – people go from their homes to get the things they need, such as visiting a doctor's surgery, attending a hospital outpatient ward, going to a day centre, visiting the dentist and so forth. (The same term could be applied to many commercial services – hairdressing, taxi services, laundry.) Then there are services that are delivered to people in their own home – cleaning, meals, help with personal care. These are 'domiciliary' services. Some domiciliary services can be provided on a separable, task-centred basis: window cleaning, gardening, decorating are familiar examples. The problems come when we assume that all personal services are like that. Take, for example, having one's teeth brushed. This is specified as one of the needs that counts as 'personal care' in Scotland,[21] and no charge is made for the service. On the face of the matter, that is a service much like having one's hair cut; but it is something that people need at least every day, and there are good reasons why people don't think of teeth cleaning in the same light as haircuts or taxi rides. Performing personal services – such as washing, bathing, teeth cleaning and hair brushing – is not a task for strangers, and certainly not a task for miscellaneous strangers.

Claims for services are often translated directly into the language of 'needs'. We talk about the 'need' for nurses, for aids and adaptations, for security, for respite care and so forth. Whenever people have particular problems, those problems might be resolved, and support might be given, in many different ways – it is not obvious, for example, whether a need for mobility is best met by personal transport, or public transport, or taxis. 'Needs' refer, in general, to the relationships between the problems people might have and the responses which are possible.

The aim of assessment, in principle, is to work out what those needs are, and to propose ways of responding to them. However, assessment serves a range of different purposes. It might be used to identify an appropriate response, or range of responses, for an individual; it could be used to allocate existing services, by determining who is eligible for help and who is not; or it might be used to plan services, taking information about (for example) how many meals on wheels are needed and using that information to provide the service. There are problems in trying to do all three at the same time; it takes time to turn plans into services, and in that time people's needs are likely to change. There are often long delays in assessments.[22] This could be coped with by a very different approach to planning: the information that is used

---

[21] Community Care and Health (Scotland) Act 2002, Schedule 1.
[22] CQC, 2020, p 25.

to develop services can be based on sample surveys, and does not have to be comprehensive or individual. Unfortunately, many current processes require people to go through lengthy assessment procedures from which individuals cannot hope to benefit, and where there is a strong likelihood that their circumstances will have changed before the response can be delivered.

The 'care package'

As a general proposition, the ways in which people's needs are met has been through identifying those needs and offering a direct response. People are either assessed for, or 'choose', the elements of a 'care package'. The idea of the 'care package' developed in the 1980s, and became the cornerstone of the 1988 Griffiths report.[23] The origins lie in Michael Bayley's seminal work, *Mental Handicap and Community Care*, published in 1973.[24] The dominant model of the time treated the formal services as central; the services they provided were extensive and supposedly comprehensive. Bayley offered a very different view of what was happening in practice. Describing the 'daily grind' of people with learning disabilities and their carers, Bayley made the case that most of the caring was being done by families and others, not by the personal social services. The work of the statutory services was, at best, complementary to the work of informal carers. If formal services were to work effectively, they needed to be 'interwoven' with the care that was actually being done, so as to meet the needs of the person and the family.[25] The idea of 'interweaving' was gradually translated into the model of a package of care. The 1988 Griffiths report explained that packages of care needed to take 'full account of personal preferences (and those of informal carers)',[26] and that they should be 'tailored ... to meet the needs of individuals'.[27]

The Griffiths scheme, introduced in 1990, never worked as intended. Part of the problem was underfunding, but that was entirely predictable. Part was the lack of support given to care managers. Evaluative studies had reported at the outset that local authorities were simply not prepared to leave a large sum of money in the hands of individual social workers.[28] Nearly thirty years later, the Feeley report in Scotland was taking complaints about the same issue: 'It's the equivalent of NHS staff having to make a case for funding every time someone needs a blood test.'[29] Part was the lack of choice actually

---

[23] R Griffiths, 1988, *Community care: agenda for action*, London: HMSO.

[24] M Bayley, 1973, *Mental handicap and community care*, London: RKP.

[25] Bayley, 1973, pp 342–3.

[26] Griffiths, 1988, para 1.3.2.

[27] Griffiths, 1988, para 6.5.

[28] A Netten, J Beecham (eds), 1993, *Costing community care*, Aldershot: Ashgate.

[29] D Feeley (Chair), 2021, *Independent review of adult social care in Scotland*, Edinburgh: Scottish Government, p 28.

available to people in practice. Part was the arrangement where assessment was divorced from service delivery, often leading to long delays – not, I think, what Griffiths intended, but generally implemented regardless. Part was the misplaced, and slightly naive, conviction that something that looked more like a market – a 'quasi-market' – would work in a context where it had never worked before. The quasi-market does seem to work for some groups, particularly mental health service users; but the apparent gains for people with learning disability are only visible once people with plans already in place are excluded, and no benefit has been shown for older people.[30] Sooner or later, we are going to have to come to terms with the realisation that this approach is never going to work fully as its advocates imagine.

The current fashion is for individual budgeting, an attempt to reproduce the kind of distribution and allocation that might otherwise be found in a private market. The model was pioneered in 1988 by the Independent Living Fund, which made it possible for people with severe disabilities to buy in the services they needed. In England, direct payments were legislated for in 1996; currently the Care Act 2014 requires local authorities to allocate personal budgets for users. In Scotland, it has been the policy since 2010 to encourage 'self-directed support'. Users in Scotland are offered four options: a direct payment to users, for them to manage; a budget allocated for the user's benefit, managed by the local authority; to receive services from the local authority; or to have some mix of the other three options. Progress has been slow, and there is some vagueness in the way that local authorities classify action, but in practice, seven years in, only 10% of the people who have been formally included in this process had received direct payments, and 75% had opted to receive services from the local authority in the usual way.[31]

In principle, individual budgeting should allow service users a degree of choice and control over the services they receive. Needham expresses some reservations:

> Personal budgets are seen as a way in which individuals can tackle some of the many limitations of existing social care provision, whether it is risk-averse professionals limiting people's choices, large block contracts proving too restrictive to meet people's support needs or private companies providing a very poor standard of care. ... The market power of individual budget holders is an inadequate force to challenge such systemic failings.[32]

---

[30] C Glendinning, D Challis, J-L Fernandez, S Jacobs, K Jones, M Knapp, J Manthorpe, N Moran, A Netten, M Stevens, M Wilberforce, 2008, *Evaluation of the Individual Budgets pilot programme*, York: Individual Budgets Evaluation Network.

[31] Audit Scotland, 2017, *Self-directed support: 2017 progress report*, Edinburgh: Audit Scotland.

[32] C Needham, 2013, *Boundaries of budgets*, London: Centre for Health and the Public Interest.

It needs to be asked whether the way that markets distribute goods and services is the right way to distribute social care. Responsiveness to the circumstances of individuals is not being done by shaping or moulding services to people's needs. It is done by offering a range of pre-existing services in different combinations. We talk about services being 'adapted' or 'tailored' to people's needs; but what this has been taken to mean is that the services are provided one by one, a little like hiring a taxi, or shopping for food in a supermarket. There are some services which can be treated like that: for example, providing a packed lunch, which can be prepared off-site and delivered at a set hour. But, for the most part, buying personal care is not like that.

The core of the problem rests in the way that private markets operate. Multiple providers compete by offering products that are comparable to their competitors' products, but sufficiently distinct to be preferable. Private services are 'commoditised': that is, they are treated as separate, distinct, substitutable commodities, which can be provided by a range of competing providers. Commoditisation is a standard element in competitive markets: it works best in theory, the OECD explain, when commodities are 'homogenous', that is, 'when they are perfect substitutes and buyers perceive no actual or real differences between the products offered by different firms'.[33] Supermarkets sell standard sizes and measures of product; hotels sell units of accommodation by the night. That is how competitive markets work. Unfortunately, the tasks of social care are not like buying stuff in a supermarket, or renting rooms in a hotel. Getting someone up, washed and dressed is not just a mechanical task, that might in the future be done by ingenious automation; it is part of a very personal set of relationships. When we see a list of commoditised care needs laid out in a contract, such as having one's hair combed or teeth brushed, we ought to recognise that something has gone wrong.

A different approach to social care

How might things be done differently? Care has to be linked to a relationship between the people involved. One side of that depends on the care workers. Caring for someone involves a degree of flexibility, and appropriate training – something the current system is not geared up to do. The people who come in to offer services, either in residential care or in someone's home, are not interchangeable; a rota of strangers can be disruptive and intrusive. If someone has to come every day to help a person get out of bed, it cannot be done every day by just one person (a paid helper has to be allowed

---

[33] OECD, 2006, Glossary of statistical terms, https://stats.oecd.org/glossary/detail. asp?ID=3230

weekends and holidays). So what is needed is a small, identifiable team of people, able to help with all the necessary elements of personal care. That calls, as a Commons committee has recognised, for 'a workforce strategy to tackle low pay, improve career development and tackle unacceptably high turnover'. Social care, they comment, is a 'people business'.[34]

The other side depends on the client. (I know that some people will baulk at the use of the term 'client'; the received jargon is 'service user' or 'customer'. But that kind of contingent, generic relationship is just the sort of thing I am trying to get away from. The relationship needs to be thought of as personal, continuing and long-term.) It is inherent in the idea of 'personal' care that the person receiving it has to be present, and that to some extent that person has to participate in service delivery. The idea of 'co-production' depends on the view that the responsibility for service delivery is shared between clients and service providers. That, Steven Osborne argues, is intrinsic to the nature of personal service. Social services do not work like supermarkets, where the supermarkets supply the goods, customers come and get them, and take them home to use. Services typically depend on a continuing relationship between the service and the client; often what is being delivered is intangible, and in almost all cases the act of provision and the act of consumption cannot be separated. It follows that users almost always have a role in the act of service delivery, and so that they are co-producers of the service.[35] Carers may need to do a range of things, which have to be negotiated with the client.

Isaacs and Neville, in a classic study, distinguished the needs of older people in terms of the timing and frequency with which the needs occurred. People could need some assistance only at longer intervals: weekly support for activities such as cleaning, household management or finance. Some people need regular and predictable assistance at short intervals: help with getting up and dressed, help with meals, help with going to bed. And some people need continuing assistance. This is not generally because they need someone with them at every second: it is because their needs are likely to be needed at 'critical intervals', unpredictably – help with continence, monitoring falls.[36]

The only needs which can be responded to adequately on a task-by-task basis are long-interval needs, such as podiatry or providing aids and adaptations. Short and critical interval needs imply frequent, personal

---

[34] House of Commons Committee of Public Accounts, 2021, *Adult social care markets*, House of Commons HC252, p 6.

[35] S Osborne, K Strokosch, 2013, It takes two to tango, *British Journal of Management*, 24(S1), S31-S47.

[36] B Isaacs, Y Neville, 1975, *The measurement of need in old people*, Edinburgh: Scottish Home & Health Department.

contact from a small group of people who the client can form a relationship with. That, in turn, implies that what people need is not a specified list of tasks, such as 'brushing hair' or 'dressing', but time with a carer – a system based, not on care as a commodity, but on carers as people. That would be very little like the system we have now.

The cost of making provision in terms of people rather than commodified tasks could be high. Labour is expensive; skilled, trained, professional carers should be expected to be more expensive still. If we had not realised before the pandemic that providing care was underpaid, undervalued and underestimated, the experience since then should have told us differently. And if there are people out there who think they will never need the service themselves, they need to think again.

Social care

Key points	The shift from health care has left services that are fragmentary, insecure and often expensive.
	Residential care has grown because it is an effective way of providing intensive services, but not all residents need that.
	Domiciliary care has been based in a flawed model of 'personalisation' – and a catastrophic assumption that it won't be sustainable.
	Care in any setting depends on continuing personal relationships.
Positive developments	This service did not exist when the welfare state was founded. It was created as part of the movement away from long-stay institutions. It has its failings, but at least it has made it possible for some people to continue to live in their own homes.
Where policy has gone wrong	Personalisation has never lived up to its promise; it only works for some.
	Creating something like a market in social care is no guarantee of choice.
	Markets offer commodities; people who need care need something different.
What to do instead	The clients of social care need people with time and skills, not a shopping list of the tasks that workers will fulfil. Both residential and domiciliary care will need teams of carers who can offer a personal service to clients.

5

Education

The foundation of the welfare state took place at the same time as the introduction of universal secondary schooling. Before the 1944 Education Act, secondary education was usually fee-paying: those who were unable to afford it continued in elementary education to age 14. But the principle of universal education had been established long before that. Primary or elementary education had been universal in Scotland since at least the seventeenth century, though the roots of the system go back before that. In England, elementary education was universal after 1870.

Schooling is meant to be inclusive – children are only permitted not to go to school if a satisfactory alternative arrangement has been made. That principle is widely respected: there are difficulties in the inclusion of some groups (such as gypsy travellers and some older pupils) but there are also provisions in place to try to ensure that they do not lose out. There have been arguments to make the provision of education more like a market, notably the idea that public provision of schools could be replaced by a system of vouchers. There are good reasons to doubt whether this would do anything to improve provision, but they need not concern us here: the main thing to note is that vouchers would still be universal, going to everyone. The principle of general inclusion – no child goes without an education – is the guarantee of universality. Universality is not compromised because some children are privately educated, though it is arguable that the quality of state education is – selective education, whether it is selected by cost or academic selection, tends to deprive less valued schools of resources. In primary education, the principle of universalism is unchallenged; the differences emerge in discussions of secondary education, where some argue for selection or different classes of education, such as a divide between vocational and academic education.

Universal education lends itself to the advancement of the general welfare. The education system operates as one of the chief forms of socialisation: education becomes a method of transmission of social norms and values. (This is also sometimes seen as a form of social control.[1]) It may serve as a 'handmaiden': the education system serves the industrial process and the economy by producing a trained workforce, and by providing childminding services. And education might be seen as a way of changing the structure of society, the class system and inequalities. The educational system provides

---

[1] S Bowles, H Gintis, 1976, *Schooling in capitalist America*, London: Haymarket.

a convenient basis for policy for children because of its universal coverage, the acceptance of responsibility for children's welfare, and because it has been easy to justify welfare measures in educational terms.[2] (It used to be common practice, too, for some services to be located in schools – school nurses, education welfare or child guidance; it was, and is, a very practical arrangement, but it has largely disappeared as those services were reorganised and re-located in different kinds of office.)

The education system

Educationists may well have learned to view education as a continuous, holistic process. That kind of understanding is often couched in terms of a general philosophy – such as 'naturalism', which argues for children to be allowed to develop by their own lights, or 'encyclopaedism', which identifies a body of learning that a scholar should engage with. Arguably, the dominant educational paradigm in British education policy has been 'liberal education': the development of each individual intellectually and socially to that person's fullest potential – but that has often been coupled with the elitist assumption, that most people's potential is somewhat limited.

The process can be thought of in terms of a system: that is, as a set of complex factors that interact with each other, and, taken together, make up a whole. However, the institutions and processes by which education is delivered have their own rationale and concerns. In institutional terms, there are different kinds of issue facing primary schools, secondary schools and universities, and attention tends to get pulled towards whichever is most prominent at a particular point, rather than the way that issues interact and affect other parts. Policy-makers, in consequence, have been likely to treat the subject of education as covering a range of fairly distinct areas – at the risk of losing sight of education as a whole process.

Primary education

The place to begin is primary education, because that is where the foundations are laid for everything else. It is the primary school that socialises pupils to work within a school environment, and establishes norms of conduct; it is the primary school that teaches foundational skills in reading, writing and arithmetic. Without that, little else can happen. Many of the problems that have been laid at the door of the secondary schools are not of their making. Many secondary schools have adapted their practice to deal with people who have not acquired the basic skills or patterns of behaviour they should have had before admission, but the

---

[2] J Finch, 1984, *Education as social policy*, London: Longman.

central point is that they should not have had to. The Moser report of 1999 commented that 'something like one adult in five in this country is not functionally literate and far more people have problems with numeracy'.[3] That figure was disputable at the time, but the core issue it is identifying is not less important for that: basic skills have to be developed at primary level. The Labour government introduced extensive testing of school children, ostensibly as a way of monitoring standards. If the exercise had really been about monitoring, a sample survey would have served the purpose. The policy was more ambitious; it was intended to make sure that no child was left behind, or 'parked' by the school. While the policy has always been controversial – parents and pupils complain about the stress that tests cause, schools complain that they are being disadvantaged by the circumstances of their intakes – there has certainly been an improvement in basic skills. There are reservations to be made about the introduction of any national curriculum, particularly when it becomes over-prescriptive, but at primary level they mainly boil down to an emphasis on reading, mathematics and science, with national tests at ages 6/7 and 10/11.

Slowly, and very gradually, the status of primary education has been increasing. The long-standing gap between expenditure per pupil in primary and secondary schools has gradually been closing: in 1978 a primary pupil cost two-thirds the cost of a secondary pupil, but by 2019 it was 80%.[4] The generally positive picture, however, has been undermined to some extent, first by the effect of 'austerity' on public spending, which has led to lower per capita spending for pupils in general, and second by the effects of the pandemic. Ofsted, the inspectorate in England, reported that children were regressing in their basic skills. They described:

> a negative impact on key stage 1 pupils' social and communication skills, listening skills, speech, phonic knowledge and gross motor skills. Regression in fine motor skills was a particular concern. … Mathematics was an area of concern for many primary school leaders. In particular, they found that pupils had fallen behind in mathematical vocabulary, place value, recall, number, fluency and data handling. Even more leaders said that pupils had lost basic literacy skills. Losses in vocabulary were frequently mentioned. … In addition, many leaders said that pupils had fallen behind and sometimes regressed in oracy,

---

[3] C Moser (Chair), 1999, *A fresh start: improving literacy and numeracy*, http://www. educationengland.org.uk/documents/moser1999/moser-report.html

[4] C Farquharson, L Siebieta, 2019, *2019 annual report on education spending in England: schools*, London: Institute for Fiscal Studies.

reading accuracy and fluency. This was having an impact on their understanding and, as a result, their confidence in being able to read.[5]

This advice was played down by the Department for Education, whose press release referred to the evidence as 'anecdotal', emphasised how well the Department was doing, and suggested only that some children would need support to 'catch up'.[6]

Schools were shut to most pupils for the best part of half the school year,[7] and often restricted in other ways. Confused messages from central government have tended to be framed in terms of making up for lost time by teaching extra material a bit faster. That seems to me to be based in a misunderstanding of what schools do, and particularly what they do at primary level. Education is a developmental process, not a matter of imparting specific knowledge in neatly definable packages. The point of insisting that every child comes to school, and that they do not take time out, is not because they will learn, on any given day, a particular thing that they must learn; it is so that they can grow, build skills, change and develop. I am sceptical that a gap of six months can be made up in an extra six months; there needs to be some additional time allowed to repair and recover the engagement and developmental momentum that has been lost. There is currently a strong case for extending the whole school career – and so ultimately, school leaving age – for a full year, supporting the millions of children whose education has been disrupted.

Secondary education

The distinction between primary and secondary education is not clear-cut; there are variations on the age when children transfer, and what they transfer to. In the time before the welfare state, children initially entered elementary education, and many would finish that education at age 12 (as my grandmother did) or later at age 14. Secondary education was fee-paying, and continued longer; private schooling often took pupils at age 13 (some still does). After the 1944 Education Act, secondary education became a regular part of the education system.

In principle, there were three types of education on offer: grammar schools, which selected pupils on the basis of an examination at age 11,

[5] Ofsted, 2020, *Covid-19 series: briefing on schools*, November, https://assets.publishing.service.gov.uk/government/uploads/system/uploads/attachment_data/file/943732/COVID-19_series_briefing_on_schools__November_2020.pdf

[6] Department for Education, 2020, *Reports on the effects of lockdown*, https://dfemedia.blog.gov.uk/2020/11/10/ofsted-reports-on-the-effects-of-lockdown

[7] L Sibieta, 2021, *The crisis in lost learning calls for a massive national policy response*, London: Institute for Fiscal Studies, https://www.ifs.org.uk/publications/15291

technical schools, and secondary moderns. The provision of technical schools was not done everywhere, and in many parts of the country the provision was effectively bipartite rather than tripartite: either children got into the grammar, or they went to the secondary modern school. When the Labour government came into power in the 1960s, they did not insist directly on comprehensive schooling, but rather sought to remove the distinction by refusing to fund further selective schools. Over time, the number of grammar schools in England fell from nearly 1300 to the present 163; more than half the reclassifications took place during the 1970s. This, however, underestimates the degree to which selection is ingrained in certain places. In Scotland, where I live, state education is nominally comprehensive – only 4% of children go to private schools – but in Edinburgh it is 25%. It is debatable whether any system can be considered 'comprehensive' if it is subject to a substantial process of selection.

The case for comprehensive education cut across a range of educational considerations about social class, opportunity and personal development. Possibly the simplest, most direct argument is found in a piece of research published during the course of the transition to comprehensive education, *Half way there*. Taking the information at a point when there were as many comprehensive schools as there were selective ones – that is, grammar and secondary modern combined – the authors could show fairly straightforwardly that comprehensives had better results than their selective alternatives. Pupils who were going to do well generally did well anyway, and those who were going to fail failed anyway. The difference was clearest at the borderlines. Pupils who had failed to get into selective grammar schools, and who went to secondary modern schools instead, did worse than those who did get into the grammar. In comprehensive schools, those pupils would emerge with some qualifications; in selective systems, they did not get the same opportunities, and so they lost out.[8]

The division between selective and comprehensive education has remained central to political debates. The 'Black Papers', a series of conservative critiques of the education system in the 1970s, argued that the abandonment of selection had been destructive, discipline in schools had been eroded, and new teaching methods had failed.[9] By contrast, the Schools Inspectorate, and Ofsted as their successor, were to make over time a very different set of criticisms of schooling: that comprehensives had imitated grammar schools instead of developing their own kind of curriculum, that exams dominated the curriculum unreasonably, and that virtually all schools let down the less able pupils. Most schools have no general problem with discipline (though Ofsted reports have commented on some deterioration in standards in

---

[8] C Benn, B Simon, 1972, *Half way there*, Harmondsworth: Penguin.

[9] B Cox and others, 1969, *The Black papers*, London: Critical Quarterly.

secondary schools). The reports do however point to patchy educational provision, some mediocre teaching, and marked underachievement of children in low-income families.[10] We should also be aware that bullying is rife – more than half all schoolchildren have experienced it[11] – and that a substantial majority of pupils and teachers report problems of stress and anxiety, particularly related to examinations.[12]

The policies that have been pursued by successive governments seem disconnected from much of this. The main developments have been:

- *Centralisation.* The Conservative government in the 1980s and 1990s introduced national assessments, and for the first time a national curriculum, shifting the locus of control from the school to the government.
- *Assessment by outcomes.* A series of measures have emphasised outcomes, measured in targets and performance criteria, rather than educational processes. This reflects a more general trend in government. The national assessments, and intermittent use of league tables, are examples. This might perhaps be justified as directing attention to pupils who are underachieving – that is the main justification for testing every pupil, rather than a sample – but it might equally be seen as a further instance of centralisation.
- *The use of 'initiatives'.* 'Initiatives' have the advantage, for government, that they allow for earmarked funding – the money cannot be used for other purposes – and that they allow governments to be selective in what they pay for and where. There has also been a plethora of further initiatives geared to greater inclusion, employability and 'lifelong learning'. There has been some criticism of potential 'initiative overload'.
- *Changing who controls schools.* A startling amount of policy effort has gone into governments' recurrent obsession with control – shifts from local authority control to nominal independence, 'leadership' and the establishment of 'academies' and 'free schools'. Sometimes these measures seem to work, but they may do so by diverting or cornering resources, displacing problems to other schools. It is debatable whether they improve standards overall.

The problems of the pandemic have highlighted one of the key problems in secondary education: the emphasis on exams. Some element of assessment and grading is probably unavoidable, both as a measure of educational

---

[10] Ofsted, 2013, *Schools*, www.ofsted.gov.uk

[11] Equality and Human Right Commission, 2019, *Is Britain fairer? The state of equality and human rights 2018*, London: EHRC.

[12] A Cowburn, M Blow, 2017, *Wise up: prioritising wellbeing in schools*, London: YoungMinds.

attainment and as evidence of skills. There is a strong case for this to be a final, 'end-stage' assessment, because doing things before the end stage works against pupils who develop or reach standards more slowly or more irregularly than others – the problem with continuous assessment. Our current exam system was built on different premises; it has two stages, rather than a single final assessment. That has come about largely because most pupils used to leave education at 16, which is no longer the case, but it has also become established as a means of permitting selective progression to more specialised study. I am sure there is a good argument for this – it will suit some pupils, as it suited me personally – but there are also good arguments for a broader education, evidenced by the use of a Baccalaureate qualification in European education and some private schools in the UK.

Tertiary education

The third major element in the education system is higher and further education. There have been several major developments: the expansion of universities in the 1950s and 1960s; the creation of the polytechnics, which became universities mainly in the 1980s and 1990s, but which started with a strong vocational and applied focus; the expansion of higher and further education, in ways which have engaged an increasingly high proportion of the age cohort of school leavers; and, arguably a concomitant of that, the expansion of postgraduate education and qualifications. Tertiary education now is mainly composed of two rather different kinds of institution: the universities, and colleges of further education. The distinction between them is not clear-cut, as universities have expanded into the provision of vocational approaches and colleges have strengthened their input into academic and professional subjects.

It may be possible to some extent to consider these developments in terms of the competing objectives of educational provision. Traditionally, universities were devoted to liberal education. The polytechnics, now 'new' universities, were meant to be vocational and arguably utilitarian. That did not last: the 'binary divide' was seen as a distinction of status as well as function. As the swelling tide of rebranded institutions indicates, the polytechnics came increasingly to do what the universities did. The colleges delivered a body of knowledge, along with vocational training, but many of them aspired to be universities, too, leading to programmes that were difficult to distinguish from higher education elsewhere. Overall, the gradual expansion of universities to occupy a mass teaching role has been accompanied by a dilution of methods rather than any fundamental redesign. To cope with larger numbers, the numbers of interactions and assessments engaged in by students have fallen. Despite the reduced emphasis on the development of skills, the grades given for degrees have also risen, with the upper second-class degree, a mark of distinction in the days of external validation, now being the norm.

The process has not been helped by a confusion, in policy circles, of tertiary education with the accumulation of knowledge. Politicians and university administrators have argued for accelerated programmes where students are taught more intensively in order to get through a degree faster – one of the key arguments for moving to 'semesters' instead of the traditional terms was that it would allow for an extra semester to take place during the summer. It is the same argument as the one being offered to make up for lost time with school closures during the pandemic, and it suffers from the same intrinsic problem: doing the same work faster or more intensively, without taking a break, is not necessarily as good as doing it slower. There are subjects where learning might be done more rapidly – I have taught some courses for practitioners on that basis – and some students who have had sufficient preparation in other settings to equip them with the skills they will need. In other subject areas, however, notably those calling for reasoning skills, the process of development calls for space, and time, and room to grow.

'Cafeteria-style' options within the curriculum are not well designed to build skills: students at that level need specialisation, development and application of the skills they learn. There is a related problem with the process of 'credit accumulation and transfer': students can be credited for work done in further education and be admitted to later stages of an undergraduate degree. The early years of undergraduate degrees are usually concerned with the development of foundational skills – mainly, in arts and social sciences, concerned with selecting, ordering and evaluating material. Moving to a different kind of learning could only work if the colleges were establishing equivalent, comparable skills. In most cases, in my experience, the colleges are doing something valuable but different – knowledge-based training, structured learning and personal development. Students who are permitted transfer and accelerated progress, on the basis of what they have done, are handicapped by the expectation that if they already know their stuff, the skills they will need to demonstrate their knowledge cannot be far behind. That does not follow.

The leading narrative: equality and inequality

Before the welfare state, the most salient educational issue was the question of inclusion. Elementary education was universal, but secondary education was not, and tertiary education was the province of a small elite; the main controversies were about what level of inclusion was appropriate for children with different aptitudes. Despite the extension of universality in the welfare state, there are still many important issues relating to inclusion – children with special educational needs and disabilities,[13] the disproportionate exclusion of some people in marginal or minority groups,[14] provision for gypsy travellers,[15] provision for migrants and those speaking English as a foreign language,[16] children in the care system,[17] and the disadvantage of some pupils with low achievement.[18] Each of these has its own history, each calls for specific policy responses, and they all matter, but a focus that did justice to all of them would not fit well in a book that is mainly concerned with broader issues.

After the 1944 Education Act, the central narrative in educational policy shifted to the issue of inequality, and to a large extent it has remained there ever since.[19] The main focus fell on the division of secondary education, where it rapidly became clear that working-class children were markedly disadvantaged relative to their middle-class counterparts. It would have been plausible to argue that this disadvantage stemmed from discrimination, stigma and biases in selection, but the evidence pointed in another direction: that the educational achievement of working-class children was simply lower, and that selection at the age of 11 mainly confirmed that. So, in the 1960s, a developing literature came to focus on the influence of the home background, and questioned how far schools could make a difference. The Head Start programme, in the USA, showed that the initial benefits of more intensive pre-school education are not maintained over time – those findings are consistent with problems that were identified in the 1960s.[20] The evidence is not favourable to those who wish to argue that early years intervention is the solution to longer-term problems.

Most of these themes have recurred in debates about inequality and low achievement – concerns not only about social class, but about race, minority groups, and children in poverty. The figures consistently show that

[13] R Long, N Roberts, S Danechi, P Loft, 2020, *Special Educational Needs: support in England*, House of Commons Library.

[14] B Graham, C White, A Edwards, S Potter, C Street, 2019, *School exclusion*, Department for Education.

[15] B Foster, P Norton, 2012, Educational equality for Gypsy, Roma and Traveller children and young people in the UK, *Equal Rights Review*, 8, pp 85–112.

[16] C Manzoni, H Rolfe, 2019, *How schools are integrating new migrant pupils and their families*, London: NIESR.

[17] M Oakley, G Miscampbell, R Gregorian, 2018, *Looked after children: the silent crisis*, London: Social Market Foundation.

[18] B Shaw, S Baars, L Menzies, 2017, *Low income pupils' progress at secondary school*, London: Social Mobility Commission.

[19] For example, H Silver (ed), 1973, *Equal opportunity in education*, London: Methuen.

[20] US Department of Health and Human Services, 2012, *Third grade follow up to the Head Start impact study: final report*, https://www.acf.hhs.gov/sites/default/files/opre/head_start_report_0.pdf

people who suffer from some disadvantage are more likely to suffer further disadvantages in the future. But they consistently fail to support the idea that people are destined to fail, or that disadvantage is inter-generational.[21]

Although many people, from all sides of the political spectrum, accept that educational disadvantage should be a focus for policy, there is a deep ambiguity in discussions as to what this actually means. For some commentators, the objective is to remove barriers to excellence – the 'career open to the talents'. This is a version of 'equality of opportunity', but it is not the only version. The problem with this particular version of equal opportunity is that people who lack the means to compete for those opportunities will still be disadvantaged. In the context of educational provision, that has been considered to imply a common educational curriculum, a foundation at least in literacy, calculations, science and language, and a general intention – not always backed up by positive measures – that no one should be left behind. Anthony Crosland, a Labour politician whose name is often associated with the drive for greater equality of opportunity, actually argued, on the contrary, that equality of opportunity was not enough. Equality was a direction of movement rather than an ideal state, but there needed to be a common foundation to ensure that everyone was able to live decently.[22] Schaar argues for a broader concept of equality of opportunity: 'the formula can be used to express the fundamental proposition that no member of the community should be denied the basic conditions necessary for the fullest participation in public life'.[23]

Education policy: a new direction

The dominant models of educational policy in UK have been different for different groups. In elite education, educational policy is often seen in terms of liberal humanism. For most of the rest, the primary objective has been instrumental and vocational. The education system serves the industrial process and the economy through a process of socialisation, the transmission of norms and values, and by producing a trained workforce. The strength of elitism in the UK is at odds with the kinds of argument made elsewhere in the welfare state. When people talk about social security spending, for example, they are likely to argue that resources should be 'targeted' on people who have the least, and object to resources going to people who

---

[21] See, for example, A Atkinson, A Maynard, C Trinder, 1983, *Parents and children*, London: Heinemann; I Kolvin, F Miller, D Scott, S Gatzanis, M Fleeting, 1990, *Continuities of deprivation?*, Aldershot: Avebury.

[22] C A R Crosland, 1956, *The future of socialism*, London: Jonathan Cape.

[23] J Schaar, 1971, Equality of opportunity, and beyond, in A de Crespigny and A Wertheimer (eds) *Contemporary political theory*, London: Nelson.

don't need it. When they talk about education, by contrast, they are likely to argue that resources are wasted when they go to people who are most disadvantaged, and that they should go to those who are better equipped to take advantage of enhanced facilities – academic learning, grammar schools and universities.

The thrust of arguments about educational policy in the UK have been concerned with disadvantage and equality of opportunity – tempered, of course, by a defence of elitism and a hefty emphasis on managerial fixes. A focus on human development could take us in a different direction. Human development is not about 'knowledge' as such, but about the skills and competences which allow knowledge to be acquired and built on. Nor is it subservient to the economy – a dangerous principle, because it implies that there may be times when development does not matter in its own right, and would need to be compromised or side-lined if the economy demands it. At every level, too, we need to be concerned about those who are excluded – left out or shut out. I mentioned before that the responsibilities of the Schools Inspectorate have been passed, in England, to Ofsted; but Ofsted has a broader remit, monitoring the work of Children's Services in local government as well as places of education, and taking in issues of child development and child protection. Consistent with that, the agenda has shifted in the direction of human development, a focus that combines elements of humanism and naturalism. The case for human development is based on a belief that everyone needs to develop, that development is a human right, and that participation in society depends on it.

When we move from the general principles to specific settings and contexts, the implications of this approach become clearer and stronger. In relation to primary schooling, it implies a focus on socialisation and basic skills – which I think many would recognise that primary schools do now. At secondary level, the emphasis falls on development, both educational and personal. A curriculum which has no place for music, art, sport or performance is an impoverished one; the objective in each case would not necessarily be to engage every child in every aspect of those subjects, but to ensure that children have the opportunities within the school curriculum to develop and grow. And then there is the problem of the final stage: assessment, qualification and transition to further or higher education. The situation calls for major reform.

Education	
Key points	Education depends on a process of development, not on any set quantity of knowledge.
	Disadvantages can be cumulative.
Positive developments	The welfare state secured free secondary education. Later developments made this comprehensive, and greatly expanded higher education.
Where policy has gone wrong	Equal opportunity is not enough; in an unequal society, it becomes the opportunity to be unequal.
	Students don't necessarily 'catch up' by being taught faster.
	The problem of low attainment is not about how schools are managed.
What to do instead	We need a stronger focus on human development. This would include a major emphasis on primary and elementary education; a review of the secondary curriculum, and reconsideration of the structure of assessment to allow for appropriate final stage qualifications.

6

Child protection

There is a general presumption, not only in Britain, that the best place for a child to grow up is in a family, and the family will be responsible for caring for that child until the child becomes an adult. The UN Convention on the Rights of the Child states that 'the child, for the full and harmonious development of his or her personality, should grow up in a family environment, in an atmosphere of happiness, love and understanding'.[1] As part of that, there are protections for family life. Raising children is a matter for parents to decide; this is treated as part of the private sphere, rather than the public domain. But there are two reservations to make about this. The first is that parents' rights are not absolute or inviolate: their rights are only a reflection of the rights of the child.[2] The second is that some families fail, and some fail in particular in their responsibilities to children.

There is no such thing as a British family policy, but there are lots of policies which might be considered to fall into the general area of 'the family'. It is probably still true to say, though less true than it was fifty years ago, that policy in the UK is based on an idealised model of a normal 'nuclear' family, in which two biological parents take responsibility for raising children. At any given time, about a quarter of all children live with lone parents. About one-fifth of children have no contact with non-resident fathers after two years.[3] (The relationship does not seem to be determined by the extent to which fathers have previously been involved with their children.) Because being single is, for many lone parents, a transitional stage, rather more children can be taken to have experienced separation from one of their parents – that may not square with the preconceptions about the norm, but it is relatively commonplace.

The implicit emphasis on the 'normal' family is evident in the presumption that children need to be with their birth family; it is also inherent in the idea that some families are doomed to fail because of their deviant behaviour or refusal to conform to social norms. There has long been a narrative which attributes a range of social problems to a relatively small number of problem families – the latest incarnation is the 'troubled family'. David Cameron, while Prime Minister, announced a new initiative in these terms:

---

[1] UN Convention on the Rights of the Child, 1989, preamble, https://www.ohchr.org/en/professionalinterest/pages/crc.aspx

[2] *Gillick v West Norfolk & Wisbech Area Health Authority* [1986] AC 112 House of Lords.

[3] T Haux, L Platt, 2015, *Parenting and contact before and after separation*, LSE/University of Kent.

'Officialdom might call them 'families with multiple disadvantages'. Some in the press might call them 'neighbours from hell'.'[4] An explanatory note from the Department for Communities and Local Government defines the 'troubled' family. Families are said to be 'troubled' if they show five of the following seven criteria for disadvantage:

1. having a low income;
2. no one in the family who is working;
3. poor housing;
4. parents who have no qualifications;
5. where the mother has a mental health problem;
6. one parent has a long-standing illness or disability; and
7. where the family is unable to afford basics, including food and clothes.[5]

Unemployed people with disabilities who are on low incomes and do not have enough money for food also find it difficult to get decent housing; that is enough in itself to qualify as a 'troubled family' by this calculation. But this, Jonathan Portes has commented, is a long way from talking about 'neighbours from hell'.

> How would you describe an unemployed single mother, with moderate depression, who can't afford new shoes for her children, and whose roof is leaking? The Prime Minister calls her a 'neighbour from hell', and argues that she, and people like her, are part of a 'culture of disruption and irresponsibility' … none of these criteria, in themselves, have anything at all to do with disruption, irresponsibility, or crime. Drug addiction and alcohol abuse are also absent. In other words, the 'troubled families' in the Prime Minister's speech are not necessarily 'neighbours from hell' at all. They are poor.[6]

There are two discrete discourses here – one about poverty, the other about families. They overlap because so many people, politicians included, tend to assume that they mean the same thing. There are undoubtedly associations between poverty and a shedload of social problems, either because poverty leads to such problems (physical and mental illness, bad housing and

[4] British Prime Minister's Office, 2011, *Troubled families speech*, http://www.number10.gov.uk/news/troubled-families-speech/
[5] DCLG, 2012, *Troubled family estimates explanatory note*, http://www.communities.gov.uk/documents/newsroom/pdf/2053538.pdf
[6] J Portes, 2012, 'Neighbours from hell': who is the Prime Minister talking about?, Blog: *Not the Treasury View*, 27 February, http://notthetreasuryview.blogspot.co.uk/2012/02/families-from-hellwho-is-prime.html

deprivation) or because social problems (such as poor educational attainment, disability and unemployment) lead to poverty. It does not follow either that poverty is the only source of such problems, or that most people in poverty present such problems: they do not. The evidence we have on low income – and there is lots of it – is that poverty is widespread, and commonplace. Most people in the UK will have experienced an extended period on low income for at least one year in the previous ten. Most of the people who experience poverty do so for only part of their lives.

Poverty does, of course, have an impact on family life. It shows itself in the prevalence of divorce, or parents breaking up; it has been argued that it also can be seen in the practice of asking relatives to care for children.[7] The possibility of separation can lead to a degree of emotional distance between family members. However, policy is often driven by a supposed link between long-term poverty and family failure. The narrative is famously expressed in terms of a 'cycle of deprivation', a term popularised in the 1970s by Sir Keith Joseph. By his account, poor parents have poor children, who grow up to become poor parents to the next generation: parents who were themselves deprived in one or more ways in childhood become in turn the parents of another generation of deprived children.[8] There has been extensive research on this issue, and it has all come to the same judgment: this is not the way that things happen. First, poor parents are not in general likely to be poor for all their lives, or even for all the time that they are responsible for children; that depends on a range of factors, such as the state of the economy. Lone parents, for example, commonly move out of poverty either by re-partnering or by moving to employment once the youngest child is in school.[9] Second, poor children do not, for the most part, grow up to be poor in their turn. They do not necessarily share the same disadvantages as their parents, but even when they do, the main routes that lead to them avoiding poverty are education, partnering – mainly, who they marry – and the economy.[10] There are higher proportions of poor children who are poor later; that is not the same thing. Third, for poverty to be passed down through the generations, it has to persist. In reality, there is constant fluctuation and attrition in the numbers, as people from poor backgrounds move to have lives which are not poor. By the time it comes to the third generation, the numbers are already far less than the numbers of people who have moved into poverty; by the fourth generation, they are hard to detect.[11]

[7] H Rodman, 1971, *Lower class families*, Oxford: Oxford University Press.

[8] K Joseph, 1972, The cycle of family deprivation, in E Butterworth, R Holman (eds) *Social welfare in modern Britain*, London: Fontana, 1975, pp 387–93.

[9] L Leisering, R Walker, 1998, *The dynamics of modern society*, Bristol: Policy Press.

[10] A Atkinson, A Maynard, C Trinder, 1983, *Parents and children*, London: Heinemann.

[11] I Kolvin, F Miller, D Scott, S Gatzanis, M Fleeting, 1990, *Continuities of deprivation?*, Aldershot: Avebury.

There are those who consider that the main focus of child protection should fall on poor children. Josh MacAlister, currently leading a review into children's social services, argues: 'We have now reached a point where the weight of evidence showing a relationship between poverty, child abuse and neglect and state intervention in family life is strong enough to warrant widespread acceptance.'[12] There are two problems with that. One is that, even if there is a statistical association, we cannot really predict where child abuse and neglect will occur. The Child Safeguarding Practice Review Panel, a body set up to take an overview of abuse in England, reports that out of 538 serious cases referred in the years since 2011, children had died in 244 cases and 294 had suffered serious harm. Of these families, 54% were known to children's services; 46% were not.[13] So the children's services miss about half of all the cases of abuse. The other issue is that poverty does not of itself predict abuse or neglect; poverty is widespread, and most parents will suffer low income at some point in the course of raising a child. It may lead to higher levels of future disadvantage, but most poor children are not disadvantaged as adults. It is much more important that poverty creates problems for the present, and those problems may imply some continued disadvantage, even if they do not imply that someone is destined to be poor. The central issue is not that poverty condemns families to fail, because it doesn't; it is that poverty is devastating, and it is devastating now.

Preventing child abuse

There are common problems which lots of children have – problems relating to poverty, education or health – but that is not what is understood as 'child protection'. The circumstances by which children come into the care of the local authority – 'looked after' children – are various, but the main categories, affecting over 80,000 children in England, are these:

- as a result of or because they were at risk of abuse or neglect – 51,780 children;
- primarily due to living in a family where the parenting capacity is chronically inadequate (family dysfunction) – 11,230;
- due to living in a family that is going through a temporary crisis that diminishes the parental capacity to adequately meet some of the children's needs (family being in acute stress) – 6,090;
- due to there being no parents available to provide for the child – 5,330;

[12] P Butler, 2021, Children's services in England shaky as Jenga tower, says review lead, *The Guardian*, 17 June.
[13] Child Safeguarding Practice Review Panel, 2020, *Annual report 2018 to 2019*, p 4.

- due to the child's or parent's disability or illness – 4,480;
- due to low income or socially unacceptable behaviour – 1,180.[14]

Most looked-after children – 72% – are placed in foster care, and 3% are adopted. Of the remainder, 15% go to residential settings, a measure which has fallen out of favour – a combination of poor outcomes with it being difficult to operate. Some (7%) remain with their parents while in care.

Child protection is mainly about protecting children from their families. The report I have already cited from the Child Safeguarding Practice Review Panel makes for chilling reading. They received 126 serious case reviews in their first year of operation.[15] They write:

> We have been profoundly disturbed by the number of serious incidents involving the non-accidental injury of babies, often resulting in their death or life-long impairment. The level of violence involved, sometimes over a protracted period, is shocking. 27% of serious incidents notified and for which we have a rapid review, involved the non-accidental injury of a baby under 12 months old. Out of 144 rapid reviews 30 reported babies had died and 114 babies survived. However, it is often the case that those who survived did so not because the serious incident was necessarily less violent, but because of the sophistication and speed of medical intervention.[16]

The argument was made influentially in the 1950s that children needed their natural mothers,[17] and this reinforced a general reluctance to believe that families could ever be the source of major abuse. In the case of physical abuse, the problems were largely dismissed until the issue was formally 'recognised' by the medical profession in the 1950s, primarily because of the work of radiologists, who were able to present X-rays of bones repeatedly broken. Sexual abuse came to prominence only after the Cleveland scandal,[18] where abuse was actively denied by the families, the consultant paediatricians were vilified, and the Director of Social Services was pressing the paediatricians not to confirm so many diagnoses of abuse. Since that time, the professions and the public have been sensitised to the possibility of sexual abuse. Many prominent cases, and cases of 'historic' abuse, have

---

[14] Department for Education, 2020, *Children looked after in England (including adoption)*, https://explore-education-statistics.service.gov.uk/find-statistics/children-looked-after-in-england-including-adoptions/2020#dataBlock-da196229-008f-4552-ba4b-a9f36430b72a-tables

[15] Child Safeguarding Practice Review Panel, 2020, p 6.

[16] Child Safeguarding Practice Review Panel, 2020, p 27.

[17] J Bowlby, 1951, *Maternal care and mental health*, Geneva: WHO.

[18] Cm 412, 1988, *Report of the inquiry into child abuse in Cleveland 1987*, London: HMSO.

come to light; and the scandal of organised sex abuse in Rotherham showed that the problems went much further than children who had otherwise been identified as 'vulnerable'.[19]

Dealing with abuse is typically the province of social work, though a range of other professions have a part in the process – doctors, nurses, health visitors, police among them. Child protection is commonly treated as a multi-disciplinary activity, with Safeguarding Children Boards (in England) or Child Protection Committees (in Scotland) working as inter-agency partnerships. Social workers who work in child protection are found in many different settings, but most in England work in Children's Services Departments, the successors of Social Services Departments, while in Scotland they will usually be part of Social Work Departments.

The basic methods used in social work rest on the premise that social workers can engage with families to bring about changes in their situation and the way they behave. Some accounts of social work see it entirely in terms of change; Martin Davies courted professional fury when he suggested in his textbook (quite rightly) that social workers were also concerned with maintaining families.[20] Social work begins with assessment: understanding what is going on in a family, how it interacts with other people, institutions and services, what will happen if nothing is done – in other words, identifying risks – and what needs to be done to lead the family in a more positive direction. This is done by problem-solving, negotiation, mobilising resources and (if all else fails) crisis intervention.

The Practice Review Panel has noted a set of recurring problems in social work practice: weak risk assessments, poor decision-making and inadequate sharing of information.[21] For MacAlister and his colleagues, 'Children's social care is gripped by a command-and-control culture'.[22] The Munro report expresses concern that the impact of successive scandals has been to produce a defensive culture in social work, along with overly prescriptive guidance which both underestimates the complexity of the issues and undermines the development of professional expertise.[23] An evaluation of the impact of a structured framework for assessment was unable to identify

---

[19] A Jay, 2014, *Independent inquiry into child sexual exploitation in Rotherham 1997–2013*, Rotherham: Rotherham MBC.

[20] M Davies, 1994, *The essential social worker*, London: Routledge.

[21] Child Safeguarding Practice Review Panel, 2020, p 4.

[22] Centre for Public Impact, 2019, *A blueprint for children's social care*, Frontline/CPI/Buurtzorg, https://thefrontline.org.uk/wp-content/uploads/2019/11/New-blueprint-for-childrens-social-care.pdf

[23] E Munro, 2011, *The Munro review of child protection: final report*, Cm 8062, London: Department for Education.

either any improvement in the quality of assessments or better outcomes for the children assessed.[24]

The development of children's services

Protecting children from abuse and neglect has been part of the welfare state from its inception, but it may be surprising to realise how little services were developed at the outset, and how much of the system we now take for granted was developed only since the 1960s. The Children Act, in 1948, came into force at the same time as the NHS and the social security system. It required local authorities to appoint a Children's Officer – typically based in a Children's Department. The Children's Departments were responsible for children in care, fostering and adoption, and residential child care. (Some other services were the responsibility of other departments: the Health Departments had mother and baby homes, maternity visiting and child guidance, while Education Departments were responsible for educational welfare.) In the first instance, Children's Departments were mainly there to rescue children after the worst had already happened, and the focus was on the care of children who had been removed from their families after abuse. The Children's Officers pressed for a broader role. They became responsible for the investigation of abuse in 1952. Developments in the voluntary sector showed how preventative work might be done in practice, and the Children's Departments finally gained the power to act to prevent abuse – the core of contemporary social work – in 1963. Bob Holman, himself a former social worker in a Children's Department, attributed three main developments to them: the recognition of the importance of children's natural parents in the process; the promotion of skills in child care; and the development of a committed (and increasingly, a professional) service.[25]

Although some aspects of child care overlapped with work with young offenders, it was only in the 1960s that the idea took hold that the origins of crime and alienation lay in 'maternal deprivation'; that young offenders needed child care, and that there should be no distinction between the services. That was the subject of the Longford report, written for the Labour Party before they came to power in 1964.[26] This argument was a motive force behind both the reform of social work in Scotland, which instituted a system of children's panels to replace the juvenile courts. In England

[24] G Macdonald, J Lewis, D Ghate, E Gardner, C Adams, G Kelly, 2017, *Evaluation of the Safeguarding Children Assessment and Analysis Framework (SAAF)*, London: Department for Education.
[25] R Holman, 1998, From children's departments to family departments, *Child and Family Social Work*, 3(3), pp 205–11.
[26] Labour Party, 1964, *Crime: a challenge to us all*, London: Labour Party.

and Wales, it led, in due course, to the 1969 Children Act, which made offending the responsibility of the personal social services, and was supposed to raise the age of criminal responsibility to 14 (that clause of the act was passed, but never activated). The law stayed in force until 1989, when the government had decided that services for young offenders should again be seen in terms of punishment.

The Social Work Departments in Scotland were formed in 1968; Social Services Departments in England and Wales followed in 1970, though it took a couple of years in some areas for the reforms to be implemented. It was signally disappointing, then, when hard on the heels of the creation of the new Departments, there was a major child care scandal. This was the case of Maria Colwell, a child who was abused and neglected by her stepfather after she had been returned to her mother from foster care.[27] Although the inquiry could be seen as a criticism of social work practice, the report was more important as evidence of major deficiencies in the procedures for dealing with child abuse. A large number of workers had known something about the case – social worker, NSPCC officer, health visitor, GP, police, housing officer – but the information had never been collated. Formally, the main legislative response to the Colwell case was the 1975 Children Act, which was limited in scope and mainly concerned with arrangements for fostering and adoption. The main innovation, custodianship, was not implemented for several years after the Act. The changes to practice were far more important. Since Colwell, the norm has been to appoint a 'key worker' to whom all information will be referred. The functions of the key worker can be divided between primary contact and role co-ordinator. The primary contact does not have to be a social worker. It could be the worker most often seen by the family – perhaps a health visitor, probation officer or NSPCC office. Role co-ordination may still be kept within social work or the Children's Services, so that other workers will refer to the right place.

The Colwell case also exposed social work to substantial criticism by the press. Child abuse is good copy – sensational, human interest, easy to relate to; it sells newspapers. Subsequent cases of child abuse have been met with extreme criticisms of social work. After the Jasmine Beckford case in 1986, the headline in the *Today* newspaper (now defunct) was: 'Social workers dance on little Jasmine's grave.' After the case of 'Baby P' in 2008, David Cameron, then leader of the opposition, complained:

> We've had a raft of excuses and not one apology. Everyone says they followed protocol to the letter and that the fault lies with some systemic failure. But we cannot allow the words 'systemic failure' to absolve

---

[27] DHSS, 1974, *Report of the Committee of Inquiry into the care and supervision of Maria Colwell*, HMSO.

anyone of responsibility. Systems are made up of people and the buck has got to stop somewhere.[28]

The Sun (not yet defunct, but working on it) was able to collect a petition of 1.5 million signatures for the sacking of all the professionals in the case.[29]

The failure to prevent child abuse has, perhaps surprisingly, had only a limited impact on policy. That reflects a painful, if implicit, acknowledgement that there is really not very much that government or professional intervention can do to stop such cases from arising. If social workers intervene actively in a family, and especially if they recommend that a child should be removed to a place of safety, they are interfering busybodies. If they fail to act, typically because the family does not cooperate, they are useless failures, or worse, morally culpable for their failure. If they do prevent abuse, it is almost impossible to prove, because it depends on showing that something would have happened, but hasn't in this case. Social workers are on a hiding to nothing. Over time, their practice has veered between an exaggerated respect for parental rights, and accusations, particularly in relation to sexual abuse, that they have been too risk-averse – that a higher standard of proof is required before taking action. A debate in the *British Medical Journal* asks whether we might have lost our sense of proportion. On one hand, there is a sense that child protection is essential, and that anything less would be 'morally indefensible'.[30] On the other, there are concerns that the focus on child abuse distracts from a range of serious, more general issues affecting the welfare of children – for example, bullying, alcohol, drugs and sex. There are concerns, too, that removal of a child may prove to be worse than abuse. The outcomes for 'looked after' children are not good, with the emotional and behavioural health of 39% identified as giving 'cause for concern'[31] – but given the damage that the children may have sustained before coming into care, it is not clear that the children's services are the source of the problem.[32]

[28] D Cameron, 2012, We've had a raft of excuses and no apology, *Evening Standard*, 13 April.
[29] Both cited in J Warner, 2014, 'Heads must roll'? Emotional politics, the press and the death of Baby P, *British Journal of Social Work*, 44(6), pp 1637–53.
[30] A Grigoire, S Hornby, M Spinelli, M Howard, 2011, Has child protection become a form of madness?, *British Medical Journal*, 342, 4 June, pp 1240–1.
[31] Department for Education, 2019, Children looked after in England (including adoption), section 3.
[32] M Oakley, G Miscampbell, R Gregorian, 2018, *Looked after children: the silent crisis*, London: Social Market Foundation.

Making things better

There have been attempts to view child protection as part of a universal framework. GIRFEC, in Scotland, stands for 'Getting it Right for Every Child'. It has been official policy since 2006, and became part of the law in 2014. The principles it stands for are, nominally, a child-centred, human rights approach; understanding children's well-being in their current situation; tackling needs early (preventatively if possible); and encouragement of joined-up working.[33] The Scottish Government had hoped that a universal approach could be applied, and one of the key ways of doing that would be to nominate a key worker for every child – a 'named person' in the event of difficulties.[34] The idea is not daft – it is based on the principle that many children, particularly those who are identified as having special educational needs, already have a named person. However, the proposal led to an explosion of dissent and derision. The larger part of the protest was directed at the prospect of interference in the family, and the concern that parents were being treated as being under suspicion. (There is also a practical objection: no service could reasonably promise continuous contact with a single named individual over a period of up to 18 years. In many local authorities, the provisions for special educational needs refer to the Director of Children's Services, or equivalent, as a place-holder for the named person; that rather defeats the purpose.)

Child protection is not a process that most families go through; it is not one that they need to go through. The process is there for the unusual cases where family fails. This is, then, a residual policy; but it is hard to envisage a society in which there will not be some need for residual child protection. It is in the nature of a residual service that there have to be criteria for selecting some people, and not selecting others. That is too often interpreted as a call to make the residual service restrictive and deterrent; but that negates the purpose of residual services, which is to mop up the conditions which are not dealt with otherwise. What should happen is that the circumstances in which the residual service is necessary should be limited, and that is done, not by limiting the service, but by changing the conditions for people who do not use the service, so that fewer come to rely on the residual safety net.

In the context of child protection, that might be taken several ways. The first task is to reduce the prevalence of physical abuse. It has long been argued that this can be done most effectively by changing the acceptability of corporal punishment – extending to children the same protections against

---

[33] Scottish Government, 2021, *Getting it right for every child*, https://www.gov.scot/policies/girfec/principles-and-values

[34] BBC, 2019, Named person scheme scrapped by Scottish Government, https://www.bbc.co.uk/news/uk-scotland-scotland-politics-49753980

being physically struck that are available to an adult. It would not mean that children never got hit, any more than the restrictions on hitting adults have stopped domestic violence; but it would remove the excuse that the amount of physical violence used was 'reasonable'. Making it illegal to hit children, the argument goes, would at least shift the curve, and that in turn would limit the number of cases where the violence caused serious harm. The case was made persuasively nearly forty years ago;[35] the Scottish Parliament brought the provision into force in November 2020.

A second option is to improve child care outside the home. Parents abuse children for a wide range of reasons, but some part of it reflects frustration, resentment and hostility when there is no respite from the endless task of engaging with a child. There are no current figures, but it is not difficult to believe that months of lockdown will be shown in due course to have led to a higher rate of abuse. Improved child care should also give, in principle, the opportunity for problems to be noticed and monitored. Social work departments have long offered nursery support to families at risk; more recently, that provision has been extended much more widely, with the extension of pre-school provision. There is still some way to go.

More remotely, perhaps, there is also a case to be made for the reduction of child poverty. The association of poverty with bad parenting is questionable, because even if there are more problems when parents are poor, the vast majority of poor parents do reasonably well or better. Obviously, it cannot help relationships in the family to have poor housing, no play space, too little money for food, not to be able to buy toys or clothes. I do not want, however, to put this case more strongly in this context; to focus on child protection, rather than the needs of children in general, is to make a relatively rare set of circumstances far more central than it ought to be. The direct case for reducing poverty is much broader, and much more compelling.

---

[35] M Sheppard, 1982, *Perceptions of child abuse*, Norwich: University of East Anglia.

Child protection

Key points	Most families raise children well enough. Some don't.
	Child protection is a residual service, for children where family fails.
	Some things can still be done for every child. The residue of children requiring protection can be reduced but not eliminated.
Positive developments	Preventative work scarcely existed when the welfare state was founded; services could only react after the event.
Where policy has gone wrong	Some families are poor, but that is not the same as saying they are not good families.
	It is not true that dependency is passed on from generation to generation.
What to do instead	Children need protection. Part can be done universally, but unavoidably part must be done individually and personally.

7

Housing

Housing is fundamental to people's welfare. First, it is something that is essential in its own right: people need shelter, warmth and space, as well as somewhere to have and do many of the other things – food preparation, personal hygiene, domestic entertainments – that are basic to well-being. Second, housing is still central to the way that most people relate to other people – making contact, interacting, sharing time, taking part in society. This role may have reduced with modern communications, but location – where the house is – still carries much more weight in valuation than the facilities that the house offers. Third, housing is the foundation for contact with other welfare services – education, health, indeed anything that depends on personal, face-to-face interactions – all organised around the place where people live.

Housing was a central element in the post-war welfare state. It had previously been closely identified with public health and slum clearance. 'Squalor' was one of the Five Giants that Beveridge had said needed to be slain. After the Second World War, housing remained a major political priority for both the main parties. What is surprising is not that housing used to be seen as a major source of welfare, but that it stopped being seen in that way. Governments came to think that it was not their business.

Housing tenure

It has been conventional, for many years, to discuss the housing system in terms of tenure: who owns the housing, and how it is paid for.

The growth of owner-occupation has been the biggest change, though it attracts less attention. At its peak, owner-occupation grew to nearly 70% of all housing; that has fallen back in recent years, reflecting the loss of resources many people have suffered through Britain's financial mismanagement and 'austerity', but most housing is owned, or is being bought, by the people who live in it.

Social housing – a general term covering both council housing, and the voluntary housing associations – developed mainly after 1919. Two million council houses were built between the wars, another four million in the post-war period. Council housing was initially intended as housing for the 'working classes'; in the 1930s, it primary role was the replacement of slums, and that meant it has always been associated to some extent with deprivation. The reduction of general needs subsidies after the 1970s meant that social housing came increasingly to serve as a residual service for people with limited resources: most tenants are in receipt of benefits. Social landlords, mainly housing associations, provide good quality housing for people who could not afford equivalent property in a market-based system. Successive Conservative governments sought to reduce the scope of the sector, at first by encouraging sales, and then, when it became apparent that many people could not hope to buy their houses at any price, by block transfers to housing associations or private renting. The finance of social housing has moved away from block grants for general needs, and now depends heavily on benefits – either Housing Benefit or its successor, the housing component of Universal Credit.

The story of private renting is more complex. Before the First World War, the vast majority of housing – about 90% – was owned by landlords, and privately rented. About 10% was owned by the people who lived there. That balance changed in part as owner-occupation grew: the building societies, mutualist and non-profit-making for most of the twentieth century, offered secure, stable, long-term finance for purchasers. That took many better-paid workers away from the rental market, and the growth of council housing took away millions more.

Private rented housing, meanwhile, was in decline: both relatively, as other sectors grew, and in absolute numbers, as the ageing properties were subject to slum clearance, or became more expensive to maintain. The demand for private rented housing never collapsed completely, but the existence of secure, less expensive alternatives meant that the main elements of that demand – the middle classes and the secure working classes – disappeared. That reduced the rents that landlords could hope to receive, and as owner-occupation increased the capital values, the landlords could get better returns by selling out to owner-occupiers. By the late 1950s, the private rented sector was in an apparently terminal condition: the stock was ageing and becoming more expensive to maintain, much of the demand for housing was being provided for by other sectors, there were better capital investments. An Act of 1957, intended to revive the sector by limiting tenants' rights, had the opposite effect: landlords took the opportunity to sell out.

Later deregulation may seem to have been more effective in revising the sector, which has greatly increased in the last ten years, but that is deceptive. For a decade, there was only limited expansion, but subsequently the combination of the economic crash of 2008, low interest rates and poor returns on investment have tilted the balance back in the sector's favour. It is still true, nevertheless, that there is precious little building for long-term private renting, and for long as that remains true it is questionable whether the sector genuinely has a future. Renting is a risky investment which locks up capital; the returns look better when interest rates are low, but as a return on capital, rental income is still very limited. If interest rates were to increase to 6 or 7% – historically, a moderate amount – landlords would need to make 9 or 10% net just to make the investment worthwhile. Rent keeps landlords afloat, but landlords make much of their money from selling up afterwards, and that will lead in due course to their leaving the market. This is not a sustainable model.

The emphasis on tenure patterns in housing policy can be a distraction, because ultimately tenure makes so little difference to the well-being of the occupiers. For example, the council houses that were sold to sitting tenants were sold on cheaply or inherited, and they have now largely become privately rented; they are still the same houses. The main difference that tenure makes, is how much the occupiers have to pay: and that matters, not because it implies that the housing is being used differently, but mainly because, in a society where low and precarious income is widespread, it also determines how much income the occupiers have for other purposes.

Housing and the market

The failures of the housing system are no longer seen directly as the province of government. Most people, the argument runs, get their housing in the private market: what matters is their ability to pay. And attention in housing policy has consequently fallen on mechanisms to enable people to command housing in a private market. The main issue nowadays, in the eyes of many if not most commentators, is affordability: making housing available that people will have enough income to pay for.[1] Contemporary disputes in housing policy typically focus on people with relatively low incomes or capital. Examples are support for first time buyers, the requirement for developers to include a proportion of 'affordable' housing in their plans, the level of rent that can be paid for by benefits, or limits on housing support imposed by the 'bedroom tax'. The implicit assumption is that housing is provided for by the market, and that any relevant intervention that needs to be made will consist of moderating or guiding the way the market operates.

In economic theory, the 'Fundamental Theorems of Welfare' purport to show that individualised markets can always do more to maximise utility, and arrange for an efficient allocation of goods and services, than general,

---

[1] See, for example, G Bramley, 2012, Affordability, poverty and housing need, *Journal of Housing and the Built Environment*, 27(2), pp 133–51; S Green, B Pattison, K Reeve, I Wilson, 2016, *How affordable is affordable housing?*, Keswick: Flagship Group; J Preece, P Hickman, B Pattison, 2020, The affordability of 'affordable' housing in England, *Housing Studies*, 35(7), pp 1214–38; G Meen, C Whitehead, 2020, *Understanding affordability*, Bristol: Policy Press.

state-based approaches can.[2] Where people have problems, it seems to follow that what matters is whether or not they can pay for something different. What is supposed to happen is that, so long as people have the money, they will choose the options that suit them best. This perspective dominates contemporary debates about housing policy; but housing, however you look at it, is different. It does not lend itself to the sort of market analysis that might work for other essentials, such as food or clothing. Markets depend on competition (which is supposed to hold prices in check, and to push producers to be efficient); very good, or even 'perfect', information; the existence of multiple suppliers; and the existence of multiple purchasers. None of this obviously applies to housing. Barlow and Duncan point to several ways in which housing markets leave the theory behind:

- *Location.* Location – where the housing actually is – is acutely important in the housing market. There cannot, because of it, be perfect information and full and free competition: houses in Birmingham are not, in any meaningful sense, part of the same supply as housing in Edinburgh.
- *Market closure.* Housing production and finance are dominated by a few major players, and this is more true in small, geographically distinct markets.
- *Externalities.* Housing both affects the environment and is affected by it.
- *Credit allocation.* The housing market is paid for mainly by borrowing, which has to be based on predictions of future value. This is very unlike the market for food.
- *Uncertainty.* Because the future is uncertain, so is the housing market. Regulation and intervention are important to reduce uncertainty.
- *The price mechanism.* Prices are set in a very limited part of the market – those who are buying and selling property at any time. Those prices are determined to a large degree by the demands of one part of the market – purchase by owner-occupiers – and the rules operated by the mortgage lenders.
- *The problem of meeting need.* If profitability is the only consideration, people will be left with needs unmet – most obviously, through homelessness.[3]

There is not a single housing market: there are many. That means that policy interventions at a national level, however well-chosen, cannot work in the same way everywhere. There will be gains and losses, winners and

---

[2] R Starr, 1997, *General equilibrium theory*, Cambridge: Cambridge University Press; and see M Blaug, 2007, The fundamental theorems of welfare economics, historically contemplated, *History of Political Economy*, 39(2), pp 185–207, http://uctv.canterbury.ac.nz/viewfile.php/users/1/8/Erskines/BlaugFTWelfareECon.pdf

[3] J Barlow, S Duncan, 1994, *Success and failure in housing provision*, Oxford: Pergamon, ch 1.

losers. It follows, unfortunately, that the idea of developing affordable private housing for everyone, housing which has a price matched to the resources of potential buyers or renters on low incomes, is a mirage; there is no way that the different elements can be brought together within the confines of a market system. No less important, this is a structure that cannot respond directly to changes in price. If more money goes into a housing market, it is distributed between competitors for scarce resources; while it is possible that more money will lead to increased access in due course, housing cannot be planned and delivered overnight, so that access can only be realised in competition with others. All our experience says that the first effect of improved market resources (mainly money) will be for those with more resources to outbid others, implying higher prices but not necessarily improved access or better housing conditions overall. And even if there was such a thing as a market equilibrium, there would be no guarantee that everyone's needs would be met.

Access to housing

For most of the last sixty years, housing policy has been skewed towards support for owner-occupiers, and residual for the poorest. The first part of that was most visible in the financial advantages available to owner-occupiers. Most of those measures have been, after a long life, phased out: they included tax relief on mortgages (which continued long after support for local authority housing had been withdrawn), the sale of council housing at a discount, and payment of mortgage interest to people on benefits. There have been intermittent schemes of support for first-time buyers, and those have been provided again recently in the form of 'Help to Buy'.

The second part is about residual provision. That is partly the result of people on higher incomes moving out, and partly the product of a greater focus on need in access and provision. It is difficult, however, to identify directly, because it describes a general trend rather than a specific set of policies. When council housing was being built in the 1930s, it was implicitly residual, because it was directed towards people who lived in slums; by the 1960s, however, the use of general subsidy had come to mean that council housing was providing secure, low-rent housing to nearly a third of the population. Conservative governments, which in the 1950s had been highly committed to council housing, had decided by the 1970s that subsidising property rather than people on low incomes was inappropriate, and that the system would be better operated in the market. The 1972 Housing Finance Act trebled rents, and introduced Rent Rebate – the forerunner of Housing Benefit – so that people on low incomes could pay the higher rents. Peter Walker, a Conservative Secretary of State, floated the idea that the government might simply give the housing to the tenants; that proposal eventually took the form of the sale of council housing at a discount. Even then, far fewer people bought their house than the government promoting the policy would have wished, and subsequent measures were taken to arrange for the transfer of housing stock to independent or private providers. The reduced provision was increasingly aimed at people in the greatest need.[4]

A range of policies at local authority level were concerned with the allocation of housing. Means-testing as such was unusual (though some councils did bar applications from owner-occupiers); much more common was the priority given to people living in overcrowded conditions, especially families with young children living in a room of a parent's house, people with young children, and people with medical problems. Legal regulation to protect homeless people had been widely disregarded in the 1960s, and the government weakened those duties in 1974; that was the background for the Housing (Homeless Persons) Act, in 1977, intended to give priority to homeless families (but not, for the most part, to homeless single people).

Provision has always been patchy. Some circumstances have been generally accepted as grounds for rehousing – being thrown out of the parental house, domestic violence, eviction – while others have not. In England, it appears that the main cause of homelessness now is loss of private accommodation.[5] In Scotland, homelessness is much more likely to reflect multiple disadvantages.[6] The focus on personal disadvantage is understandable, because that is part of the everyday life of people who are looking for secure housing, and the housing managers who are trying to provide for them. It does, however, disguise the extent to which this is a structural problem, not a personal one. The immediate reasons why people cannot find a secure home to live in are not the product of their personal disadvantages or failings. Other people with problems of mental health, unemployment and family breakup might well have somewhere to live; that depends on the resources they have, the people who may be able to support them, and of course the accommodation that is available.

What is true is that wherever there is scarcity, the people who are least able to compete, for whatever reason, lose out. In a classic study, Clapham and Kintrea found that the process of assessment for housing allocations in Glasgow favoured people on higher incomes, even though there were no questions asked directly about their income. People on relatively higher incomes tended to start off in better accommodation than people on lower incomes. They had fewer points given for housing need, but more for

[4] I Cole, R Furbey, 1994, *The eclipse of council housing*, London: Routledge.

[5] LGIU Homelessness Commission, 2019, *Final report*, London: LGIU.

[6] B Reid, 2021, *Preventing homelessness in Scotland*, Edinburgh: Homelessness Prevention Review Group/Crisis.

waiting time. The effect of making an allowance for waiting time was that the people who could get the better offers – the property that was more in demand, which needed more points to be considered – were the people who could manage in what they had, and who could wait for a better offer.[7] The system effectively produced a set of conditions in which the inequalities of the market occurred in a non-market setting.

There has been a tendency in present-day politics to treat the issues surrounding housing as if they were 'pathological', the problems of individuals and families. Nowhere is this more visible than in the discussion of rough sleeping. When I have asked support workers about the needs of homeless people, they tend to say that these people needed emotional support, training and life skills. When homeless people are asked themselves, they are likely to say that they are cold and hungry.[8] Rough sleepers may well be slower, poorer, more damaged than other people. Many have lost the support of family. Some have mental problems. None of those is the main reason that they have nowhere to live. To understand what is happening, it might help to draw an analogy with a game for children: musical chairs. The object of the game is to sit down on a chair as soon as the music stops. Some children are faster than others; some are stronger; some cheat. And some children get left out; often the slowest, weakest or youngest. But the central issue, the reason why some children will find nowhere to sit, is that there are not enough chairs. At the outset of the COVID-19 crisis, the authorities were able to find ways to keep people off the streets. As lockdown eased, they stopped doing it – and when lockdown happened again, many did not bother. The key issues are not about personal behaviour, but about resources and access to housing. These issues are 'structural', the product of the way that resources and access are organised: they reflect the rules of the game.

The real housing problem

For much of the period between 1945 and 1970, the main emphasis in housing policy fell on housebuilding. Crudely, the numbers of households – groups of people who could be expected to live together, such as nuclear families – exceeded the numbers of dwellings, or 'units of accommodation'. This comes from Labour's 1951 manifesto:

> We shall maintain the present rate of 200,000 new houses a year and increase it as soon as raw materials and manpower can be spared. Most

---

[7] D Clapham, K Kintrea, 1986, Rationing, choice and constraint, *Journal of Social Policy*, 15(1), pp 51–68.

[8] P Spicker, J Love, L Strangward, P McLaverty, P Strachan, 2002, *Homeless in Aberdeen*, Aberdeen: Centre for Public Policy and Management, Robert Gordon University.

of these houses will as now be built for rent and not for sale, and for the benefit of those whose housing need is greatest.[9]

The Conservative election manifesto outbid them. It explained:

Housing is the first of the social services. It is also one of the keys to increased productivity. Work, family life, health and education are all undermined by overcrowded homes. Therefore a Conservative and Unionist Government will give housing a priority second only to national defence. Our target remains 300,000 houses a year.[10]

Housebuilding remained a priority through the 1960s.

Once the number of dwellings exceeded the numbers of households, politicians came to think they could rest easy – the main outstanding issues were house condition and affordability, not housebuilding. In that, they were mistaken, and we are still living with the consequences of that mistake. After nearly fifty years of seriously inadequate housebuilding, we are suffering major shortages, a severe maldistribution of housing resources, and a problem with disrepair that reflects an assumption that housing never wears out.

Working out how many homes are needed is not as straightforward as it might seem at first. The definition of both houses and households is open to interpretation. One of the things that happens whenever new accommodation becomes available is that new households form as people move into it. 'Household fission' occurs when people who used to live together move into separate dwellings – for example, when people divorce, or when a young person leaves home to set up independently. Both patterns have been increasing in recent years. Mulhern argues that the number of households has not kept pace with the number of houses;[11] I am not persuaded. At the same time as he makes that claim, he also notes the existence of 400,000 'hidden households' in England, a round number which may be an underestimate as well as an over-estimate. Household formation and household fission depend on the number of dwellings that are available for those to use, and availability depends in turn on both supply and cost. As long as there are not enough houses that people can afford to occupy, the potential number of households will not be realised.

---

[9] Labour Party Election Manifesto, 1951, http://www.labour-party.org.uk/manifestos/1951/1951-labour-manifesto.shtml

[10] Conservative Party General Election Manifesto, 1951, http://www.conservativemanifesto.com/1951/1951-conservative-manifesto.shtml

[11] I Mulheirn, 2019, *Tackling the UK housing crisis: is supply the answer?*, UK Collaborative Centre for Housing Evidence.

The count of houses, or properly speaking of dwellings, is also an uncertain guide to need. In the first place, it includes housing that is unliveable, or, as the legal phrase puts it, 'unfit for human habitation'. Some intolerable housing is capable of repair; much is not. This is not a very clearly defined category either, because public health officers have to get permission before they can add property to the list, and no local authority wants to classify its housing stock as unliveable if it cannot do anything about it for the next twenty years.

Next, the count includes property that is not available for people to use as housing. Typically, that is because it is owned and used by someone else – second homes and holiday lets. One of the reasons why household formation does not seem to keep pace with construction is that second home use does not create a new household.

Third, we need some houses to be empty: a 'vacancy surplus', because without it, people would find it very difficult physically to move house.

Fourth, some housing is just in the wrong place. The houses that are unoccupied in Dundee aren't much use to people who can't find accommodation in Cornwall. It's difficult enough for people living in Luton to commute to Cambridge, or vice versa, and those places are less than forty miles apart. This problem is sometimes referred to coldly as a 'locational deficit', and the numbers of houses that fall short is the sum of all local shortages. Mulheirn disputes that this is happening, because the same patterns apply across different English regions;[12] but this is about locality, not regional difference. The houses we live in are not just spaces that we fill; they are the centre of our social connections, the way we get to work, to school, to play and to interact with other people. William Julius Wilson writes, from the USA, about the differences between the people who move out and the people who stay; the appearance of the 'ghetto' has a lot to do with differential patterns of movement, between those who have the option to leave and those who don't.[13] Some houses are in places where people don't want to live, but in other places there will be shortages.

There is more than one kind of problem here, but the implications of this simple analysis are stark. We do not in the UK have enough places for people to live – and we need to be aware that, even if we build, the release of pent-up demand will mean that the people who are most in need are not necessarily those who will be able to occupy places that become available. The Lyons Review argued that in England there are simply not enough houses:

---

[12] Mulheirn, 2019, p 12.
[13] W J Wilson, 1987, *The truly disadvantaged*, Chicago: University of Chicago Press.

For decades we have failed to build enough homes to meet demand. We need to build at least 243,000 homes a year to keep up with the number of new households being formed, but last year we only built 109,000 homes. Indeed, we have only managed an average of 137,000 homes a year over the last ten years. Without a change of course, it is predicted that the country will be short of up to two million homes by 2020.[14]

A House of Commons Select Committee argues more specifically for building social housing for rent:

A social housebuilding programme should be top of the Government's agenda to rebuild the country from the impact of COVID-19. The crisis has exposed our broken housing system. Families in overcrowded homes have faced worse health outcomes. Private renters have struggled to meet housing costs. ... It is time for Government to invest.[15]

The consequences of inadequate housing supply are problems of access, and problems of deprivation. The problems of access principally affect those who are looking for alternative housing at any point, but clearly that is also going to include people who are currently in housing that is in some way inadequate for their needs.

The shortage of housing has major implications for people's lives. As housing becomes available, some people have the resources to claim it, and others will be left behind. The people who are likely to be excluded are the people who have least. Where access to housing is governed by the price of the housing, the people who are left behind are going to be people on low incomes, but the process is more complex than this – and more pervasive. The quality of housing people are able to occupy depends on their ability to choose, and the same is true of deprived areas of towns and cities. People who have least choice end up in the places least to be chosen.

The scarcity of decent housing, in the right place, means that people will have to find some other way to live. They may have to share with relatives or friends – that is where most 'hidden' households are to be found. 'For every two people who are sleeping on the streets, there are 98 who are homeless but hidden from view.'[16] When I worked in a local authority housing department, I met (literally) hundreds of families living in the spare rooms of their parents' houses. Homeless people may find themselves placed

---

[14] The Lyons Housing Review, 2014, *Mobilising across the nation to build the homes our children need*, London: Digital Creative Services, p 6.

[15] House of Commons Housing, Communities and Local Government Committee, 2020, *Building more social housing*, HC173, pp 33, 39.

[16] LGIU, 2019.

in a hotel or bed and breakfast – many local authorities still use these. They may have to live in some of the unfit housing, with all the problems that entails. They may have no shelter at all. People are homeless because they have nowhere to live. If there are not enough places, some of them have to use accommodation which is unfit or unsuitable; some will be physically homeless. It is simple arithmetic. Nothing can be done effectively without a very major increase in housing supply.

The problems of poor areas

There is a tendency for many social problems – problems such as poverty, unemployment, low educational attainment and crime – to be 'concentrated' in poorer areas. Concentration does not mean, in the UK, that everyone is deprived, or even that most people are; it means only that there is a greater likelihood of deprivation there than elsewhere. Deprivation is widely dispersed. Most poor people do not live in poor areas; most of the people living in poor areas are not themselves poor.

When we talk about poor areas, or areas of multiple deprivation, it generally means not simply that there are more poor people there, but that there is something about the area that disadvantages the people who live in it. The problems of these areas are compounded by the lack of communal resources – poor transport links, underfunded public facilities, lack of commercial services. These problems are not confined to people in those areas who are individually poor; they affect everyone who lives in the same place. That means, in turn, that these places are not places where many people want to live. There are no 'ghettos', but there is a higher prevalence of all sorts of deprivation: people with resources can choose not to live there, or to live somewhere else, and people without resources may not have the option.

The issues afflicting deprived communities have largely been dealt with in three ways. First, there have been policies devoted to specific services, such as Educational Priority Areas (which were actually focussed on individual primary schools), housing improvements or employment initiatives. Second, there has been 'regeneration' – usually implying some decision to change the people living there – for example, by demolishing unpopular estates or redeveloping property for other uses (such as housing for older people, or for owner-occupiers). And then there have been 'community' initiatives, intended to work with communities which have little sense of community: community development, which tries to mobilise people around better facilities; community organisation, which tries to empower people; and community education which tries to build social capacity and skills.[17]

---

[17] See G Craig, M Mayo, K Popple, M Shaw, M Taylor (eds), 2011, *The community development reader*, Bristol: Policy Press.

The benefits of community-based approaches are hard to gainsay – a neighbourhood which has a community garden, a community library or a play area is generally a better place to live than it was when it did not have these things – but they are usually marginal at best. There is just as good an argument for trying to ensure that there is a pleasant living environment and decent facilities everywhere – poverty is widely dispersed, and there are poorer people even in the richest places. Dispersing problems can help to overcome one of the central issues, which is the risk of a living environment that undermines welfare; but the risk of 'regeneration' in these terms is that, when deprived places become less deprived, the problems will simply be shifted to some other place.

A broader approach

We need more housing, but that is still only part of the problem. We have to think more broadly: not just about the spaces that people live in, but how those spaces shape their lives. If housing is a focus for participation in society, social life and the delivery of services, we need to be aware how that works, and what we can do, if not to make people's lives better, at least not to make them worse.

Much of this discussion tends to be treated as if it referred primarily to concentrations of deprivation in particular areas of towns and cities – that is not the same problem as the ones I am discussing here. The South East of the country is overpopulated, much of the North is economically depressed, and other areas have lost population to the point where schools, hospitals, shops or services cease to be viable. Faced with so much housing that is in the wrong place, we have two options. One is to move people away from places that can't sustain their populations. *The Economist* has suggested that we should shut down some of Britain's failing cities[18] – places like Burnley, Hull and Hartlepool. They argue that they can't be saved; that keeping them going is expensive and hopeless; that the best thing the residents can do for themselves is to move out; that the best thing for government to do is to let big cities grow while these places shrivel and die. But there are reasons to care about these places. They cannot offer some of the things that other places can – particularly, economic prospects and opportunities. However, they have their own attractions. Hull has two universities and has been a UK City of Culture. Hartlepool is well located by the coast, there's good access to major facilities in the big towns, it's reasonably well served by rail and road, and some parts are lovely even if the economic decline

---

[18] *Economist*, 2013, The urban ghosts, 12 October, http://www.economist.com/news/britain/21587799-these-days-worst-urban-decay-found-not-big-cities-small-ones-urban-ghosts

isn't. The failing towns, so-called, have their own established communities, the places where people live, grow up, live with their families, meet their friends and form the ties of everyday life. That's precious, and difficult to replace. Beyond that, they have a wide range of valuable resources – houses, roads, infrastructure, schools and so forth – which would otherwise have to be replaced. It's not the strongest objection, but the proposal to shut down these towns is puzzlingly profligate.

The other option is to move the facilities and opportunities to the places where people live – moving work, improving communications, developing transport links, creating more infrastructure rather than less. 'Moving work to the workers' was the policy of the Labour government in the 1960s, long since abandoned in the belief that the market would sort things out. But leaving the distribution of population to the market has been tried for most of the last fifty years, and it hasn't sorted things out – they've got worse. The idea of planning (sometimes diminished to 'urban planning') is liable to be dismissed nowadays: a Policy Exchange report questions whether an assessment of the need for future development can have any practical foundation.[19] Some overblown claims by urban planners – based on the confident assumption that planners controlled and guided the use of collective resources[20] – have given way to the rather strange idea that planners are mainly there to adjudicate in disputes about land use, and that they have to act as if they were courts of justice. We are more aware of past failures – large, out-of-town estates with no facilities – than of the relative success of other planned communities, such as the garden suburbs. The combination of limited powers and strong economic currents has meant that planning has tended to work best where it is able to guide or steer development – as it did in the regeneration of Docklands in East London – and not so effectively where it goes against the flow, such as the attempt to save town centres as areas for shopping. This is a complex process, and the right answers can be difficult to identify. That has been the rationale for a greater degree of local decision-making – backed up by the resources that local communities need.

The issues around housing stretch far beyond housing itself: they touch on every aspect of people's lives, and beyond that to issues of community, society and the economy. There is no sovereign remedy for all of this, but we know where it has to start, because it is where the welfare state started: build more houses, provide more social housing, manage the spatial distribution of resources and opportunities – and this time, don't stop.

---

[19] J Airey, C Doughty, 2020, *Rethinking the planning system for the 21st century*, London: Policy Exchange.

[20] D Eversley, 1973, *The planner in society*, London: Faber and Faber.

Housing

Key points	People have to live where they can. If there are not enough houses, some people will live in unfit housing, some will have no home of their own, and some will be physically homeless.
Positive developments	The legacy of post-war policies has been a greatly improved and expanded housing stock.
	Social housing continues to provide essential, good quality housing to those who cannot afford adequate housing within a market-oriented system.
Where policy has gone wrong	The housing market does not work in the way that free-marketeers imagine.
	The issues of tenure and affordability disguise the real issues: access and deprivation.
	The problems of the housing system are structural, not the result of individual failings.
What to do instead	We need a substantial, continuing increase in the stock of housing, in order to ensure access and adequate standards.
	A programme of regeneration is needed to save towns and regions that have been marginalised.

8

Employment services

The employment services sit rather uncomfortably between two opposed understandings about what a welfare state should do about unemployment. One of those is structural: employment and unemployment are determined by the state and structure of the economy. Beveridge identified a range of factors which contributed to unemployment: some was seasonal, some casual, some 'frictional' – the delay in moving to new work; but much was cyclical, depending on the general state of the economy.[1] Full employment was presented, in the Beveridge report, as one of its key 'assumptions' – a policy that was necessary if the rest of the scheme was to work.[2] At the time, there were grounds for confidence that unemployment could be dealt with. Governments knew, thanks to the ideas of John Maynard Keynes, what they needed to do to secure full employment, and it worked. In a White Paper in 1944, the wartime coalition committed the governments that would come after them to do so.[3] Britain had full employment, more or less, for the best part of twenty-five years after the war. Governments eventually abandoned the policies which had brought that about because they felt that other economic objectives – growth, inflation and the creation of a 'flexible' economy – were more important.

The other main approach is individualistic: employment and unemployment depended on the actions and choices of the people affected. That attitude was prevalent in the nineteenth and early twentieth centuries, but it was substantially discredited by the experience of mass unemployment between the wars. It was to resurface despite the resurgence of mass unemployment in the 1980s, and much of the effort to deal with unemployment has been directed at the choices and behaviour of unemployed people. The trend was reinforced by the Labour government, which in 2002 changed the name of the Department of Social Security to Work and Pensions, brought employment services into the same ministry in the form of 'Jobcentre Plus', and subsequently introduced 'welfare reform' intended to spur people into work.

In the course of the last fifty years, there has been a bewildering range of initiatives and programmes, often short-lived, intended to improve the situation of people who are unemployed. There has been an 'alphabet

---

[1] W Beveridge, 1944, *Full employment in a free society*, London: Allen and Unwin.
[2] W Beveridge, 1942, *Social insurance and allied services*, London: HMSO.
[3] Cmd 6527, 1944, *Employment policy*, London: HMSO.

soup' of agencies – for example, the Job Creation Programme (another 'JCP'), the Manpower Services Commission (MSC), the Special Temporary Employment Programme (STEP), the Youth Opportunities Programme (YOPs), the Community Enterprise Programme, Employment Action (EA), the Training Opportunities Programme (TOPS), Technical and Educational Councils (TECs), Restart, the Enterprise Allowance Scheme (EAS) and many more. Some were for younger people, some for adults. Some created jobs, some offered training, some offered advice and support, and some supported employers – to take people on, to have people stay, to have them leave, possibly to stabilise the position of businesses. The scope and scale of these measures made it seem unreasonable not to include them in a review of the welfare state. But the measures have often been localised and time-limited, and it is difficult to see them as part of a coherent, national service. The provision has often been scrappy, the coverage incomplete, and the programmes ephemeral.

Some of the things that employment services do are residual and individual: the support for people who have been marginalised by the labour market, the disciplines visited on people who are long-term unemployed, the emphasis on writing job applications rather than equipping people with employable skills. The individualised approach has come to dominate in recent years, because of the powerful link between employment services and conditionality in the benefits system. However, other aspects of the employment services are institutional: there is a general acceptance by governments that they have some responsibility to mitigate the damage caused by unemployment. Examples include the creation of opportunities for training and retraining; the special measures taken during the pandemic to maintain people's links to the world of work, and measures to provide work experience. (The insensitively named 'Kickstart' programme only provides for 20,000 young people at present,[4] but the plan is to extend its provisions – work placements of six months, paid for by the government – to half a million.)

There is a place for personal assessment and support, particularly for people who are furthest from the labour market. The methods used by employment services relate to individual assessment, ways of enhancing personal development. A range of measures can help people who are economically excluded; they include preparing people – building confidence, resilience and networks; developing the skills that the labour market is looking for; filling gaps in their CV; and overcoming barriers, such

---

[4] N Rigby, A Sinclair, 2021, Kickstart: concerns over delays in young unemployed job scheme, *BBC News*, 23 May, https://www.bbc.co.uk/news/uk-england-norfolk-57191289

as caring responsibilities, disability and location.[5] The range of approaches is an indication of the seriousness and expertise of the field; but generic skills do not address the primary problems that unemployed people face, and the barriers are not resolvable by individual action. The primary determinant of whether people find work is the state of the economy, and if more jobs are available, more people will be able to work, even if they have begun at a disadvantage.

It has to be said, beyond that, that most unemployed people do not need this kind of support at all. Most unemployed people left to their own devices will find work regardless.

Active labour market policy

There has been, Deacon and Patrick argue, a political consensus on welfare policy. It is based on the central propositions that employment can transform people's lives, in a way that benefits cannot, and that benefit claimants have to be directed accordingly.[6] Since the 'welfare reforms' of 2008 and after, national policy has largely focused on people who were held to be insufficiently engaged in the labour market – a discipline which has been applied fairly indiscriminately across a spectrum ranging from those who are passing through a relatively brief, transitional interruption of earnings, to people who are so incapacitated that it would be 'unreasonable' to expect them to work – that is what the points scheme for incapacity is supposed to assess. The accusation was that national policy was 'passive', simply accepting the position of unemployment without expecting that people would move into work. David Freud, a banker invited to advise the Labour government before he became a Conservative minister, wrote:

> Passive labour market policies gained ascendancy in the late 1960s as the UK, in common with many major economies, increasingly sought to achieve its goals through full employment fiscal policies. The requirement for labour market attachment was reduced ... It was with the introduction of Restart interviews and a stricter availability test in 1986 that the UK made a clean break with the passive welfare state of the previous twenty years. This was the start of a long process of re-engagement with the long-term unemployed to give them a second chance at finding work. In the years that followed, the benefits

[5] Learning and Work Institute, 2016, *Scotland's future employment services*, Leicester: LWI, http://www.employabilityinscotland.com/media/519601/scotlands_future_employment_services_-_literature_review_-_cesi_-_january_2016.pdf

[6] A Deacon, R Patrick, 2011, A new welfare settlement?, in H Bochel (ed) *The Conservative Party and social policy*, Bristol: Policy Press.

regime for the unemployed has become increasingly active, and the foundation of the present structure was established.[7]

Given the range of employment initiatives I have already referred to, this was alarmingly ill-informed – at best ignorant, at worst cavalier in its disregard of the lessons that might have been learned from previous experience. That did not make it less influential: policies were introduced to make unemployed people more 'active', which generally meant that they should run faster in the race to become employed. It is questionable whether 'active' policies of this type have yielded any practical benefits. Before welfare reform, people registered as unemployed would have been expected to look for work, and hardly anyone would be continuously unemployed for as long as five years. There is some evidence to suggest that the imposition of the Work Programme acted to slow down the rate at which people return to work.[8] The agencies selected to provide the service were overwhelmed by the large number of referrals, and there were accusations that where they were not cherry-picking or 'creaming' those people who were likely to find employment anyway, they were throwing other people arbitrarily at available jobs in the hope that some would stick.[9] The closing set of figures for the Work Programme, in 2017, showed a gradual improvement; about one-third of the people referred to the Programme are placed in work, 5% more than the 27% who might otherwise have been expected to find work.[10] Those figures predate the pandemic and the disruption it has caused. The Work Programme has now been superseded by the Work and Health Programme, and most of the referrals coming to it are people with disabilities. Of the first 150,000 referrals, there have been 'job outcomes' for 10,000.[11]

The Work Programme was supposedly aimed at people who were disengaged from the labour market, and were unlikely to move into work. That applied to very few people who were healthy or who did not have caring responsibilities that prevented them working – and arguably, to a minority of the people who were actually referred to the programme. The Social Security Advisory Committee has been critical of the emphasis: 'Low levels of benefit and the DWP's "work first" approach can encourage

---

[7] D Freud, 2007, *Reducing dependency, increasing opportunity*, London: Department for Work and Pensions, p 12.

[8] J Portes, 2012, http://notthetreasuryview.blogspot.com/2012/02/work-experience-does-it-work.html

[9] House of Commons Work and Pensions Committee, 2013, *Can the Work Programme work for all users?*, HC 162.

[10] Department for Work and Pensions, 2020, *Work Programme statistical summary: data to June 2020*, https://www.gov.uk/government/statistics/work-programme-statistical-summary-data-to-june-2020

[11] A Powell, 2020, *Work and Health Programme*, House of Commons Library Briefing 7845.

individuals to take any job, rather than one well-matched to their skills and experience.'[12] That criticism was particularly focused on the response to the pandemic, but it applied throughout the period of 'welfare reform'. Before 2008 and the renewed focus on engagement with the labour market, people who were incapacitated would have been exempt from conditions attached to work, and large numbers would receive incapacity benefits for long periods before they formally entered retirement. (The test for incapacity was aimed to identify people who it was 'unreasonable' to expect to work; at least, that is what the law said.) Now many have been placed in a group which requires them to be 'work ready', and they receive long-term training that will prepare them for the call, if ever they are fit enough to answer it.

This process has been overlain with the issues around the commissioning of private provision, but the central flaw lies in the way that the policy has been conceived; private providers cannot do impossible things. The satirical journal *Private Eye* described the Work Programme as 'marred by poor results, corruption, exploitation of the unemployed and the collapse of leading providers'.[13] 'Corruption' is a bit harsh. The rules were bent to keep the providers on board, but this was a failure of policy, not a diversion of resources. The government had hoped that the programme would lead to people moving to the labour market in large numbers, and planned to pay agencies by results. When this did not happen, the agencies either gave up or threatened to, and the government redefined the terms of their contracts because otherwise the system would simply have folded.

The emphasis is falling increasingly on policies that have little to do with 'unemployment' as it used to be understood. The DWP currently estimates that expenditure on benefits for unemployed people will more than double next year, and nearly treble by 2025–6.[14] That estimate seems to depend, not on a prediction of economic catastrophe, but on a process of reclassifying people who are incapacitated as if they were looking for work. The statutory conditions for incapacity benefits explain that they are there for people who it is 'not reasonable' to expect to work, and the tests they are subject to have been designed on that basis.[15] About half of these people will be asked to undertake 'work-related activity'. At present the only criterion used to determine whether people are capable of such activity is an assumption that by default people who are sick but need less support ought to be expected to participate. So they are set to do things like writing a CV and invited

[12] N Timmins, G Tetlow, C Emmerson, S Brien, 2021, *Jobs and benefits: the Covid-19 challenge*, London: Social Security Advisory Committee/Institute for Government, https://www.gov.uk/government/publications/jobs-and-benefits-the-covid-19-challenge/jobs-and-benefits-the-covid-19-challenge

[13] *Private Eye*, 2021, Gravy train restarts, issue 1539, 4 February, p 7.

[14] Department of Work and Pensions, 2021, *Benefit expenditure and caseload tables 2021*.

[15] Welfare Reform Act, 2012, section 37.

to have their confidence built. Sick people can work, but the point of the support they receive is to ensure that they should not have to. Requiring sick people to meet work-related commitments is neither reasonable nor likely to achieve any useful purpose.

The employment services have been tainted by their identification with the benefits system, and the compulsory extension of the process to hundreds of thousands of people who would have found employment without them. The fatal flaw in the policy stems from the contemptuous assumption that people who are out of work are insufficiently motivated to do things for themselves, and they will not work without being directed to do it, trained to apply for jobs, disciplined through penalties or otherwise being 'encouraged'. Engagement with the labour market is treated as a matter for individuals. There is more than enough evidence to say that, on the contrary, unemployment is mainly a reflection of the state of the economy.[16] The way to lead people into jobs is to make sure that there are jobs on offer for them to move to, and that they have the training and skills that are needed. If people need specific skills to work, they will not necessarily be the sort of 'soft' skills that employment services have concentrated on: they are much more likely to be specific to certain occupations in short supply, such as child care, adult social care, and nursing. That is a task for education and manpower planning, not 'activation'.

However, there are also major problems with the kinds of jobs that are available − not just for people who are unemployed. In the post-war period, there was a general concern about what was called a 'dual labour market', where people would be trapped for their whole working life in low-paid employment. With the decline in manufacturing, much of that employment has disappeared; but it has been replaced with a return to low-paid, insecure and casualised work, on terms which had mainly been left behind after the First World War. The bulk of jobs newly created since 2008 have been taken by people who are disadvantaged, such as people in minority ethnic groups, people with disabilities, migrants and the low paid, but two-thirds of those jobs have been on poor terms − self-employment, zero-hours contracts or agency work.[17] The government's pursuit of a 'flexible' economy has been interpreted in terms of employers' ability to hire and fire; that has been supported by an erosion of rights, for example through the growth of bogus self-employment or zero-hours contracts. What the European Union calls 'flexicurity' looks a lot like precarious labour.[18]

---

[16] S Clarke, 2019, *Setting the record straight*, London: Resolution Foundation.

[17] Clarke, 2019, section 2.

[18] M Simms, 2009, *United Kingdom: flexicurity and industrial relations*, https://www.eurofound. europa.eu/publications/report/2009/united-kingdom-flexicurity-and-industrial-relations

The labour market in theory

The individualised assumptions about labour have been translated in economic theory into a model where employment and unemployment are understood in terms of supply and demand. The labour market, in classical economics, consists of a series of transactions, where workers decide whether to offer their services, and employers decide whether or not to buy them. The wage rate – the price of labour – can be used to bring the supply and demand for labour into an 'equilibrium', at which point there will be full employment, defined as the position where everyone who wishes to work at the going wage will be able to do so.

It is difficult to present this as if it was a coherent narrative, because it is far removed from reality. Most people of working age in Britain participate in the labour market. They do not 'decide' whether to work or not; work or the prospect of work is part of everyday life. Most unemployed people find work within a year, and while some will not, year by year, even most long-term unemployed people find work; those who do not are mainly ill, disabled or effectively retired. Most workers have no opportunity to negotiate about wages or hours, and even if there is an 'equilibrium', there is no reason to suppose that everyone who is looking for work will get it, or conversely that anyone who wants to employ people will find the people to do the job.

Keynes, in one of the most influential economics books of the last century, made two key points. First, the level of employment or unemployment is primarily determined, not by the actions or choices of individuals, but by the level of activity there is in the economy as a whole. If the economy is depressed, so will be any demand for labour. Second, there is no reason to suppose that a stable level of activity which happens to apply in any particular economy will be one that offers full employment. Nor is there any reason to suppose that the private sector will expand spontaneously to do it.[19]

It might be argued that the model of the labour market in terms of supply and demand is still useful – that it offers predictions of general trends. But if this was true, we should expect the following propositions to guide us.

- If wages increase, the supply of labour will increase, because people who are not engaged in the labour market will decide to apply for jobs; and the demand for labour will fall. The belief that minimum wages would lead to increased unemployment is based on this analysis – but particularly on the effect of the demand for labour, which starts from the premise

---

[19] J M Keynes, 1936, *The general theory of employment, interest and money*, London: Macmillan.

that if wages rise above a minimum, employers will find it too expensive to employ people.[20]

- If wages fall, the supply of labour will fall. Charles Murray argues that if people have the option of remaining on benefits, the rational thing to do is not to work.[21]
- The supply of labour will also be responsive to changes in returns brought about by government intervention. If benefits or taxes increase, the marginal return from employment will fall, and so will the supply of labour. People will choose to work less, or not to work. Conversely, if benefits or taxes decrease, the return from employment will increase, and so will the supply of labour.

There is plenty of supportive theory, but the evidence is thin, and what there is does not necessarily back up the theory. Part of the difficulty in finding convincing confirmation has been that, despite the strenuous efforts of economists to prove the link, the effects tend to be marginal. There are relatively few circumstances where decisions about working and not working might be determined by such effects: the differential between benefits and wages is wide, the conditions attaching to benefits are restrictive, there is little scope for employees to vary the terms of employment, and in any case most choices can only be made at points of transition – when people are moving from one kind of employment status to another. This leaves little room for examples where existing incentives might be decisive. Even if the effects are there, they may be cancelled or averaged out by other behaviours that lead in contradictory directions: if some people are discouraged from taking on extra work by higher taxes, which is uncertain, they are counterbalanced by those who feel the need to work more to reach a target income. And overall, there is very little relationship between the level of benefits in a country and participation in the labour market. On the contrary, as a general proposition, countries with higher levels of benefit also tend to have higher labour market participation; that may well be because both of those things point to economies where incomes are higher.

The larger part of the problem with the evidence, however, is hard-wired into the way that conventional empirical social science tries to use it. Researchers attempt to isolate the effects of different variables, 'bracketing off' factors that might muddy the analysis. Economists usually work to the assumption that 'other things are equal': they never are. The factors that get bracketed off – issues like family circumstances, the range of opportunities, the position of women, the impact of disability, the pursuit of alternatives

---

[20] *Economist*, 2020, What harm do minimum wages do?, 15 August, https://www.economist.com/schools-brief/2020/08/15/what-harm-do-minimum-wages-do

[21] C Murray, 1984, *Losing ground*, New York: Basic Books.

like education, the influence of culture – are often the ones that we most want to know about. When it comes to employment, probably the single most important factor to consider is the state of the economy – something that is side-lined whenever the analysis depends on observations within the same economy, such as differences between the states of the USA. And looking at employment as if it had no social context, for example by focusing only on the difference that benefits might make to decisions about taking a job, ignores most of the other things that matter – differentiation in the labour market, domestic arrangements (such as spouse's employment or arrangements for child care), the ability that any individual person has to apply for the jobs that are on offer (such as qualifications, physical capacity, domestic arrangements such as the position of spouse or the availability of child care, location and alternative options), and of course the state of the economy and whether there are any jobs to apply for. By the time all of that is taken into account, the theoretical predictions of classical economics don't do a lot to tell us what's really going on.

Work and social security

For the best part of forty years, policies relating to employment have been dominated by a paradigm which sees the issue of unemployment mainly as a matter for individuals, who make choices about whether or not to work. That has led to a central focus on social security benefits, which are seen as crucial to those decisions. Benefits are represented as offering a disincentive to work – people will not work, the argument goes, if they get money for doing nothing.[22]

This is generally translated into a concern that no one should be better off on benefits than they would be in work. The common-sense interpretation of that phrase might be that people should get less on benefits than they could get if they were working, but in the UK, the proposition is understood differently: it is usually translated into a much more stringent principle, that no one on benefits should be better off than anyone who is working. These are not equivalent. The first, that people should not be better off on the dole, is about personal incentives. In France, unemployment benefits are related to the previous earnings of the unemployed person, and reduce over time on the basis that someone who is unemployed for longer periods should expect less when they are ultimately re-employed.[23] That is not what we do in Britain – there is no earnings-relation, and beyond that, claimants can be penalised if after three months they are not ready to take much lower

---

[22] See, for example, Murray, 1984.

[23] Unédic, 2021, *Vos questions*, https://www.unedic.org/indemnisation/vos-questions-sur-indemnisation-assurance-chomage/mon-ancien-salaire-brut-mensuel

paid work. The second, more stringent proposition is that no one should be better off than anyone who is working. The principle of 'less eligibility', expounded in the Poor Law Report of 1834, argued that the situation of the pauper 'on the whole shall not be made really or apparently as eligible as the independent labourer of the lowest class'.[24] That is not concerned with whether or not any particular individual is better off, but with other principles altogether – partly about the perceived fairness of rewards for working and not working, and partly (as the authors of the Poor Law report believed) the protection of the relative position of poor labourers. The effect of making people better off by not working was supposed to force up the price of labour, leading to unemployment. It is more obvious, with the benefit of hindsight, that this is just not true – making workers better off is the key to a booming economy. That doesn't stop people from spouting the same nonsense nowadays.

The narrative goes something like this. People can take advantage of the generous benefits system to decide not to work. They might not have worked for years, and there are families in Britain where no one has worked for generations. These people have to be encouraged, or pushed, to take work. Where they lack the skills that employers need, they have to be educated to become employable. Carrots and sticks work.[25]

This is all untrue, in every way that matters. First, the benefits system in the UK is particularly ungenerous: it offers a very low 'replacement ratio'. Several countries have both more generous schemes, by the same test, and higher rates of participation in the labour market. (Some studies present a higher replacement ratio by including support for housing costs; but that support is also available to people in work.)

Second, long-term dependency on unemployment benefits (as opposed to other benefits) is exceedingly rare. There are people who receive other benefits for long periods – pensions are the obvious example – but the numbers of people who are 'job seekers', that is, people of working age who are unemployed, and remain continuously on benefits, are very small, and only a minuscule proportion of those people who pass through spells of unemployment.[26] The vast majority of longer-term recipients are chronically sick or disabled; a smaller cohort are single parents, mainly women, with young children at home. Currently the government presents people as long-term unemployed if they have not worked for three years out of the preceding four. The test is largely based on people who have recently been in employment, not people who have 'never worked'.

---

[24] S Checkland and O Checkland (eds), 1974, *The Poor Law report of 1834*, Harmondsworth: Penguin.

[25] Murray, 1984.

[26] See P Spicker, 2011, *The length of claims*, http://blog.spicker.uk/the-length-of-claims/

Third, if there are any families where no one has worked for generations, they are difficult to spot. There are certainly families where three generations might all be out of work at the same time, because families still tend to live near each other (or even in the same place) and they could all have been hit by economic depression at the same time. However, the numbers where each generation has had the same experiences as the last are tiny, and by the third generation this is vanishingly small. A research project which set out to investigate inter-generational unemployment in Glasgow and Middlesbrough, both areas of relatively high unemployment, couldn't find any examples. They compared the search to the hunt for the Yeti.[27]

Fourth, although there is evidence that some people won't work when work is available, it refers to a modestly sized minority, and it is somewhat mixed. The largest group of people who do not move from benefits to work are people with incapacities – mainly serious illness, and disabling conditions which lead people effectively to retire. There are people in certain situations who opt not to work when they could – women with child care responsibilities are less likely to work if their partner is out of work; and there are jobs that are difficult to fill – for example, seasonal agricultural work, which offers an unappetising combination of low wages, insecure employment, inaccessible sites, lack of compatibility with family responsibilities, and physically demanding work.[28] By contrast, the growth of the 'gig economy' shows that millions of people have taken up employment in jobs with poor conditions, protection and prospects, just so long as they are in accessible locations and can be reconciled with other responsibilities.

The final point is about sticks and carrots. Carrots are in short supply, but we have seen lots of sticks recently, in the form of sanctions for failure to seek work with sufficient vigour or penalties for refusing offers of employment. Private firms have been hired to encourage people to be 'employable'. This has all been a pretty miserable failure. There is no evidence to show that people on these programmes are more likely to work than those who have been left to find a job for themselves, and some to suggest that the effect of these interventions is to get in the way of people finding a job.[29] The experience of sanctions is that they have been used liberally, but that they are mainly used not to get people into work more effectively, but to penalise them for failing to turn up in time for meetings with officials – that accounts for nearly 90% of all sanctions in 2019, more than 200,000 people who

[27] R McDonald, T Shildrick, A Furlong, 2013, In search of intergenerational cultures of worklessness, *Critical Social Policy*, 34(2), pp 199–220, doi: 10.1177/0261018313501825

[28] L O'Carroll, 2020, British workers reject fruit picking job as Romanians flown in, *The Guardian*, 17 April, https://www.theguardian.com/environment/2020/apr/17/british-workers-reject-fruit-picking-jobs-as-romanians-flown-in-coronavirus

[29] HC 162, 2013.

lost their benefits for a month or more.[30] If we really want more people to participate in the labour market — given the numbers of those people who are seriously incapacitated, especially among older males, it is not obvious that we should — the first thing to do is not to get out the whips, but to have some jobs to offer them.

How to make jobs

Full employment is not produced spontaneously by the economy — we learned that in the 1920s and 1930s. If governments want there to be full employment, they have to act to bring it about. Keynes pointed to the benefits of a programme of public works: 'Pyramid building', he wrote, 'earthquakes, even wars may serve to increase wealth'.[31] Gold mines might look like a complete waste of everyone's time, setting people digging for something that they couldn't make much use of, but the economic activity they generated was something to be valued. Writing with tongue firmly in cheek, Keynes continues by suggesting that governments could create something that was as good as a gold mine:

> If the Treasury were to fill old bottles with banknotes, bury them at suitable depths in disused coal-mines which are then filled up to the surface with town rubbish, and leave it to private enterprise on well tried principles of laissez faire to dig the notes up again ... there need be no more unemployment and, with the help of the repercussions, the real income of the community ... would become a good deal greater than it actually is. ... It would, indeed, be more sensible to build houses and the like; but if there are political and practical difficulties in the way of this, the above would be better than nothing.

Keynesian economics did what it promised. Most governments in developed countries had full employment for thirty years after the war — they dropped the policy for other reasons, mainly to do with the (misunderstood) relationship between Keynesianism and inflation. But since then, classical economics — the same set of theories that stopped most governments acting effectively in the 1920s and 1930s — has been resurgent; governments have shown themselves willing to accept, and even to encourage, mass unemployment in the pursuit of other objectives; and a myth has taken hold: that government can't create jobs. The World Bank's World Development Report 2013 claimed, for example, that 'it is not the role of governments to

[30] D Webster, 2020, *Briefing: Benefit sanctions statistics*, Child Poverty Action Group, June, pp 11–12.
[31] Keynes, 1936, p 129.

create jobs ... as a general rule it is the private sector that creates jobs'.[32] This comes from ideology, not the real world. We need more police, doctors, cleaners, teachers, janitors, street and park wardens, nurses and carers. Those are genuine jobs. The private sector does not create them spontaneously, but governments can create them by design.

There are three good reasons to expand public employment. The first is economic: it is better for people to be working than not. Unemployment is wasteful and unproductive; it costs money to keep people out of work. People can only pay tax if they are earning. The second reason is that it is better for the people who are employed. We need to invest in our people. Instead of punishing people for not finding work that isn't there, we could reward them for doing the work that we create. Third, there are things we need to happen. We don't have enough houses for the population. Our services for older people and mental health are woefully short of trained staff. We don't have enough child care, and what we have is fantastically expensive. Our public spaces are crumbling – if we invested more in builders, plumbers, painters, gardeners or people to mend roads, it would do a power of good.

So – how should we go about it? The political parties like to pluck figures from the air – a million jobs, two million. This is not a good way to go forward. We know that 10,000 public sector jobs will be better than none, that 50,000 will be better than 10,000, that 500,000 will be better than 100,000, and so on; the point at which it stops is either when there is nothing left to do, or when there are not enough people to fill the jobs that are being created. But we also know that jobs need to be resourced, that people need to be trained, and that we want to be sure that money is being spent in the right places. The idea of increasing the number of public sector jobs is based on a principle, rather than a target, or any ideal number. The best answer about numbers is this: we need more than we have now. We shouldn't stop expanding the public sector till the task is done.

---

[32] World Bank, 2013, *World development report 2013: jobs*, Oxford: Oxford University Press, p 21.

Employment services

Key points	The level of employment is mainly dependent on the economy, not on individual effort.
	At their best, employment services offer support and training to help people engage with the labour market; but they cannot create jobs or guarantee decent employment.
Positive developments	Where macroeconomic policies have been applied, they have greatly diminished the level of unemployment.
Where policy has gone wrong	'Active' labour market policy shifts the burden of responsibility for unemployment to the people who experience it.
	Incentives are not a simple matter of comparing benefit levels with wages.
	The standard microeconomic analysis, presenting unemployment as a matter of personal choice, is an ideological prejudice, not social science.
	Employment services have suffered by being muddled with benefits.
What to do instead	Unemployment is a waste of human resources. We need large numbers of people in a range of professions. Government can, and should, create jobs. It can do this through expanding public employment.

9

Equalities and human rights

Work with 'equalities' was not part of the original conception of the welfare state, but a focus on some equalities has since become part of the institutional structure. It is true that major pillars of the welfare state were built in part with the intention of dealing with inequality, mainly understood either in terms of class (as it was in housing and education) or income; and it is also true that other aspects of inequality, notably inequalities in health, have become part of the agenda. 'Equalities', for all that there is much about the term that overlaps with inequality of those kinds, address a somewhat different set of issues.

Inequality rests in a relationship of advantage or disadvantage. Saying that people are 'unequal' is not the same as saying that they are different; it is a statement than some of them have an advantage over others. A claim for equality between the sexes, for example, does not mean that everyone should be the same sex; it means that women should not be disadvantaged relative to men. And a claim for greater equality for disabled people does not mean that everyone should have the same capacity; it means that people with disabilities should not suffer greater disadvantage because social life is not arranged with them in mind. The pursuit of equality is about the removal of disadvantage.[1]

There are however two key differences between the general concept of 'equality' and the specific practice of 'equalities'. First, 'equality' can be, in Rae's terms, 'individual-regarding' – looking at the status of each and every person as an individual – or 'bloc-regarding', looking at whole groups such as women, minority ethnic groups or LGBT groups.[2] Some of the debates about inequality are mainly concerned with the position of individuals and families – examples are debates about poverty, or living wages, or housing conditions. The main focus of 'equalities', by contrast, is bloc-regarding. When we think about such issues as the disadvantage of women, we are comparing one bloc – 'women' – to another group – 'men'. A woman with high income may seek to have disadvantage corrected; a man with lower income may not be able to. So, we can reasonably consider, under the heading of equalities, a range of issues where the problem is that relatively powerful women do not have the same advantages as relatively powerful men – issues such as the 'glass ceiling', the representation of women in parliament,

---

[1] See P Spicker, 2006, *Liberty equality fraternity*, Bristol: Policy Press.
[2] D Rae, 1981, *Equalities*, Cambridge, MA: Harvard University Press.

or the presence of women on the boards of major companies. That remains true even if those women are relatively advantaged in individual terms, relative to poorer men or other women.

Second, policies for 'equality' are much broader than policies for 'equalities'. Equalities have mainly been concerned with equal treatment – treating people as equals – and equal rights. The protections offered to disadvantaged groups are not necessarily concerned with inequalities in provision, in outcomes, or in well-being. We know, or we ought to know, that Muslims in the UK are subject to potentially extreme prejudice, and that they are likely to have lower incomes, poorer health outcomes and shorter life expectancies than others do;[3] but the form of equality that is being emphasised is an attempt to stop discrimination, not to address any of these other problems. With the main exception of equal pay for women, there is not much said in debates about 'equalities' that argues for general action against poverty. There are then other, potentially competing concepts of equality, which place more emphasis on substantive outcomes. To achieve basic security, or access for everyone to the conditions of civilisation, it may be necessary to discriminate in favour of disadvantaged groups and communities. Equality of welfare is also concerned with substance, rather than process; when people express concern about inequalities in health, they are usually thinking about how best to improve people's health, not how to eliminate prejudice and discrimination. Equal treatment is important, but it falls a long way short of substantive equality.

Institutional racism

Institutional racism is not the only issue being addressed by equalities policy, but it describes an important set of issues in its own right, and in many ways it has become a model for the response made in relation to other inequalities, including legal redress, the identification of unconscious bias, and institutional practice. When the term first came into use, the intention was to refer, fairly generally, to the racism endemic in American society. The term has been used in the same general sense in Britain, but after the Stephen Lawrence inquiry, it came to be used far more often as a critique of formal institutions.[4] Stephen Lawrence was a London teenager, randomly murdered in a racist attack because of his colour. The police failed to respond appropriately while he lay bleeding to death; subsequently they failed to investigate the murder, put together the evidence or arrest

---

[3] T Modood, R Berthoud, J Lakey, J Nazroo, P Smith, S Virdee, S Beishon, 1997, *Ethnic minorities in Britain: diversity and disadvantage*, London: Policy Studies Institute.

[4] Cm 4262-1, 1999, *The Stephen Lawrence inquiry (the Macpherson report)*, London: TSO, http://www.archive.official-documents.co.uk/document/cm42/4262/4262.htm

the murderers. Much of this was described as the product of 'institutional racism' by the Macpherson report, but some of the evidence offered by investigating officers might better, if more crudely, be described simply as 'racist'. (The inquiry report, rather too leniently, described overt racist prejudice as 'unwitting' when the officers were unable to see the racism in what they were saying.) More than twenty years after Macpherson, we have had 'Black Lives Matter', and abundant evidence of continued racial harassment and intimidation by the police of British people going about their everyday lives.

The Inquiry described institutional racism as 'the collective failure of an organisation to provide an appropriate and professional service to people because of their colour, culture or ethnic origin'.[5] It has four main elements: prejudice, either open or covert; direct discrimination; discriminatory processes – such as the aggressive use of 'stop and search'; and the systemic production of disadvantage, which may be explicit and intentional (such as the deliberate exclusion of immigrants from dependency on public funds) but could also be indirect, an accumulation of disadvantages. There is a common distinction drawn between direct and indirect discrimination. It is direct when there is a deliberate action which puts people at a disadvantage: for example, recruitment practices which exclude people on the basis of their personal characteristics. It is indirect when something about the rules acts to limit opportunities, or close them off altogether.

There is a long history, for example, of the production of racial disadvantage in social housing allocations. Disadvantage can arise in a number of ways. It is often difficult to obtain access to the list: residential qualifications are less of an issue than they used to be, because many minority applicants are long-term residents in an area, but there are still problems of obtaining the information to apply; restrictions relating to immigration status and 'dependency on public funds' can be used to screen out applications. The range of property available has not always been suitable for minority groups, either because of location or household composition. The effect of policies for dispersal has been to reduce the range of property available to tenants, which leads to delay. The criteria for rehousing disadvantage applicants from minorities. Minorities are often concentrated in certain parts of the private sector, particularly in private rented housing and low income owner-occupation, which are given low priority in many allocation schemes. The selection of tenants, and matching them with properties, provides an avenue for discrimination, whether deliberate or not. It is arguable whether any of these factors is crucial in itself, but taken together, the effect of these policies in producing disadvantage is substantial.[6]

---

[5] Cm 4262-1, 1999, para 6.34.
[6] See, for example, S Smith, 1989, *The politics of 'race' and residence*, Brighton: Polity, ch 4.

A much-derided recent report on racism in Britain claimed that there was no institutional racism in Britain, in the sense that institutions were not following policies that were racist or discriminatory.[7] This was a misunderstanding of the term, and of the process; the production of systemic disadvantage does not have to be the result of deliberate policy to qualify as institutional racism. By contrast, a powerful synoptic report from the UK parliament, from a joint committee of both houses, identifies a range of institutional disadvantages experienced by 'BAME' (Black, Asian and Minority Ethnic) people. Disadvantage and minority status are not adequately summed up in terms of skin colour, and the categorisations bring together people from a disparate range of cultures and backgrounds. The report focuses, within a wide range of potential concerns, on three diverse and somewhat different groups of 'Black' people: African British, Caribbean British, and people of mixed race with connections to either group. Three quarters of survey respondents from those groups feel that their human rights are not well protected by comparison with the 'White' or majority population, and they are right to think that. Black communities are over-policed, and 85% of respondents are concerned that they will be treated worse than a White person. Black citizens are under-represented in the democratic process: 25% are not registered to vote, against 17% in the general population. The death rate for Black women in childbirth is five times that of the rest. The risk of death from COVID-19 is something between 10% and 50% more than others.[8] There is rather more to be said on inequalities in health. A study in the *Lancet* identifies a stark difference in the health and mortality of a range of minority ethnic groups: 'We estimated wide inequalities ... (affecting) Gypsy or Irish Traveller, Bangladeshi, Pakistani, and Arab groups similar to, or exceeding, the decrement associated with a two-decade difference in age.' Beyond that, there is also a marked difference in the quality of care these groups receive. 'Ethnic inequalities ... were accompanied by increased prevalence of long-term conditions or multimorbidity, poor experiences of primary care, insufficient support from local services, low patient self-confidence in managing their own health, and high area-level social deprivation.'[9]

I think it is fairly evident that the problems run deep, that they are complex, and that they are cumulative. It may be possible, through a series of legal challenges, to whittle down the range and scope of discriminatory

---

[7] T Sewell (Chair), 2021, *Commission on Race and Ethnic Disparities: the report*, https://www.gov.uk/government/publications/the-report-of-the-commission-on-race-and-ethnic-disparities

[8] House of Commons and House of Lords Joint Committee on Human Rights, 2020, *Black people, racism and human rights*, HC559.

[9] R Watkinson, M Sutton, A Turner, 2021, Ethnic inequalities in health-related quality of life among older adults in England, *The Lancet Public Health*, 28 January, p 1.

processes and the production of disadvantage. But there are some problems considered here that are not going to be touched by an approach which focuses centrally on equal treatment. Even if rights relating to non-discrimination were affirmed and enforced to the greatest extent possible, there would still be problems that were not being addressed.

The legislation

The roots of current legislation can be found in laws governing discrimination on the grounds of sex (the 1975 Sex Discrimination Act) and race (the Race Relations Acts, a long series beginning in 1965). Laws about disability (the Disability Discrimination Acts of 1995 and 2005) and age discrimination (the 2006 Act) came later. The main issues that these laws have in common are concerned with discrimination – not prejudice as such, but the disadvantage that results from unequal treatment.

The 2010 Equality Act[10] follows a progressive extension of the criteria to include other groups. The Act prohibits discrimination, harassment or victimisation for people with a range of 'protected characteristics', and requires a public service 'when making decisions of a strategic nature about how to exercise its functions, (to) have due regard to the desirability of exercising them in a way that is designed to reduce the inequalities of outcome which result from socio-economic disadvantage'. It also requires public services to make reasonable adjustments for people with disabilities.

The protected characteristics are:

- age
- disability
- gender reassignment
- marriage and civil partnership
- pregnancy and maternity
- race
- religion or belief
- sex
- sexual orientation

There are gaps and ambiguities here. The terms are open to interpretation, but it is not certain as things stand whether there is enforceable protection for people whose gender is intersex or non-binary, whether chronic or terminal illness is adequately covered by 'disability', whether discrimination against lone parents can be said to be covered by 'marriage and civil partnership', or whether people of Irish descent are a minority ethnic group (they do

---

[10] https://www.legislation.gov.uk/ukpga/2010/15/contents

suffer the disadvantage of one[11]). There is shocking discrimination directed towards travellers, and there are major failures of service,[12] but the limited protection offered under equalities legislation is confined to sub-groups within the traveller population – mainly Romany gypsies, Scottish travellers and Irish travellers. Possibly the holes will be filled in as cases are considered by the courts, but it is difficult to say that with confidence.

Beyond the limitations of the categories, there are other inequalities which are left out: national origin (anti-European prejudice, currently directed at Romanians and Bulgarians, has resurfaced), locality or the discriminatory effects of positive prejudice towards others (favouritism for people who have been to public school, who are members of a club, or co-religionists). In Belgium, equalities legislation refers to inequalities of birth, and inequalities of 'fortune' – being unlucky is not a good enough reason for people to be homeless or destitute, or a reason to differentiate between people.

The bulk of the protections that are on offer concern non-discrimination, though the provision for disability sometimes goes further in offering positive remedies. Inequalities are mainly addressed by offering individuals the right to seek redress in a court of law. Hartley Dean has identified a range of problems associated with attempts to establish social rights through the courts. There is a long-standing tension between legal and social policy approaches: legal theorists have been concerned that the law might be over-socialised, while social policy analysts have been concerned that the process might be over-legalised. Generic social policies are not enough, because they cannot offer redress when things go wrong; but legal approaches have substantial limitations. Courts can be expensive, and slow. The legal approach can extend the scope of social rights, but it can't make the resources available to prevent disadvantage from arising. The process can reveal evidence of policy failure, but the courts do not have the final word on policy. The approach can empower individuals, but it can also leave it for individuals to resolve issues that might otherwise be considered collectively.[13] The courts in Britain do not allow mass class actions, of the sort which are made frequently in the USA; nor in most cases do they accept generalised academic and statistical evidence about the effect of a practice or policy, which in America would be the subject of a 'Brandeis brief'. Effectively, this means that most cases tend to be framed in terms of how the individual who is suing has been treated: it takes a brave, firm and arguably an articulate person to become a figurehead.

---

[11] M Clucas, 2009, The Irish health disadvantage in England, *Ethnicity and Health*, 14(6), pp 553–73, http://wrap.warwick.ac.uk/16812/

[12] H Cromarty, 2019, *Gypsies and Travellers*, House of Commons Briefing Paper 08083.

[13] H Dean, 2015, *Social rights and human welfare*, London: Routledge, ch 8.

There is, usefully, an alternative route. The Equality and Human Rights Commission (EHRC) monitors and regulates action in relation to equalities. It can support litigants directly, but it can also issue pre-enforcement notices, or itself join in a legal action. As a regulator, its enforcement powers include the power to take injunctions, to ask for action plans, to make assessments, to negotiate agreements and to require compliance, subject to fines. They have tended to issue about a hundred notices, and take action themselves in about ten cases every year. There has been some concern that the very broad remit of the EHRC has led to a less focused and effective approach in relation to 'race' than the previous Commission for Racial Equality had.[14] O'Cinneide points to the substantial limitations of the process: the EHRC is constrained, like similar organisations elsewhere in Europe, by resources, political interventions and legal restraints on its powers, as well as the inherent limitations of attempting to work with excluded and marginalised groups. He argues, nevertheless, that the EHRC can act as a catalyst, and an agent of change.[15]

Dealing with discrimination is important, but narrow. If disability or child care interrupt someone's work record, limiting discrimination is not going to make up for the disadvantage. Some of the disadvantages arise from other factors. Single people and adult couples find it much more difficult to get housing than parents with children, because most social housing was built with three bedrooms; half the housing lists in Scotland are taken up by single people, and very little of the accommodation available will be allocated to them. That is not going to change because discrimination has been removed on the basis of sexuality. And sometimes the disadvantages that people experience are cumulative, in terms of past opportunities, salary, contributions to pensions, or experience; removing discrimination here and now is not going to make up what has been lost.

The other main part of the legislation is the attempt to push equalities on to the agenda. 'Mainstreaming' has three components: the acceptance of key principles, the development of systems to deal with inequalities, and the use of tools such as equality impact assessments.[16] In principle, this should mean that agencies are constantly aware of the importance of equalities. However, the practice falls some way short of this, and the success of this type of measure is open to question. The treatment of impact assessments, at both central and local government level, is often cursory, with civil servants and local government officers 'ticking boxes' and often claiming that important

---

[14] Joint Committee on Human Rights, 2020, p 32.

[15] C O'Cinneide, 2016, The catalytic potential of equality and human rights commissions, *Journal of Poverty and Social Justice*, 24(1), pp 7–20.

[16] F Mackay, K Bilton, 2003, *Learning from experience: lessons in mainstreaming equal opportunities*, Edinburgh: Scottish Executive.

areas of policy, such as economic planning or benefits administration, raise no equality issues. More straightforwardly, the EHRC attempts to keep equalities in the public eye by regular publication of information, in a series entitled, 'Is Britain Fairer?'[17] The reports range over a huge range of social issues, including work, education, justice, poverty and social care.

Human rights

In the UK, equalities have tended to be elided with human rights – reference to one is often taken to be a reference to other. The essential similarity between equalities and human rights – and arguably, the reason for the narrow reading given to both – is that they are treated as being open to litigation by the individuals, and sometimes by the groups, who are affected by them. Human rights legislation can be taken to define a set of principles, offering minimum standards of treatment in key areas such as justice.

Human rights apply to everyone, and it follows that they are also implicitly, and sometimes explicitly, egalitarian. The Universal Declaration of Human Rights states, in its first article, that 'All human beings are born free and equal in dignity and rights'.[18] There are references to equal rights in relation to equal pay for equal work, marriage and divorce, voting rights and access to public services. However, the 'rights' in human rights are not rights to equal things. Article 17, for example, is concerned with the right to property: 'no-one shall be arbitrarily deprived of his property'. (A great deal there hangs on what is 'arbitrary'. The Duke of Westminster, who owns much of Belgravia in London, sought in 1986 to claim that giving rights to his leaseholders was an infringement of his human rights. He lost.)

Human rights fall some way short of protecting people from the consequences of inequality. In the first place, human rights are universal. That is not intrinsically a weakness, but it does restrict their scope. Many of the rights that people have in our society are particular rather than general. Rights to social security, especially pensions, are often based on contributions and personal work record; some of the rights are subject to immigration status and residence. Rights of inheritance reflect the nature of family life and the wishes of the deceased person. Rights to housing often depend on relevant contracts, not on the welfare of the people who live in the houses.

Second, human rights are basic – they define only the minimum that should be expected from a government. A recent judgment in the European Court of Human Rights upheld the right of a Roma woman to beg, on

---

[17] Equalities and Human Rights Commission, 2019, *Is Britain fairer?*, https://www.equalityhumanrights.com/en/britain-fairer

[18] United Nations, 1948, Universal Declaration of Human Rights, Article 1.

the basis that the right to beg was an expression of her dignity – but the right to have enough resources not to need to beg is not protected.[19] The limitations of human rights law are more easily understood when we set human rights against the 'thicker', fuller and more extensive, rights associated with citizenship. There used to be a right to a minimum income in the UK – sadly, that is no longer true for people below pension age – but it was never a human right. People who are homeless are (supposedly) entitled to priority for rehousing by a local authority; that is not a human right. People in the UK have rights to health care, including both acute care in a crisis and long-term continuing care. This, too, is not a 'human right' – it goes far beyond it.

Third, human rights are sketchy – they outline general principles, not specific measures. There is, for example, a right to social security, but nothing about what sort or level of social security should be offered; a right to rest and leisure, but not to have somewhere to sleep or a place to take leisure; a right to a decent standard of living, but not to have what one needs to wash or a place to sleep. It can reasonably be argued, and it often has been, that once these standards have been established in a particular society, taking them away becomes a breach of human rights. Getting to that stage is problematic.

Human rights advocates in international organisations have argued, for many years, for a progressive extension in the scope of human rights. Much of this is done under the general title of 'economic, social and cultural rights', which are mentioned in the Universal Declaration of Human Rights[20] but have until relatively recently had only a marginal role. The United Nations has slowly adopted provisions to support – among others – people with disabilities, children and indigenous peoples,[21] and it has developed guidance relating to poverty even if that is not yet clearly recognised as a human right.[22] The focus on indigenous peoples is particularly interesting, because it does acknowledge that the disadvantages that people experience may be collective, not just the position of individuals. However, the enforcement of human rights in the UK is still heavily dependent on action in the courts, and UK courts tend to take a very individualistic approach. Despite the fuss that has been made about the Human Rights Act, which incorporates the European Convention of Human Rights into UK domestic law, very few judgments have been made which have held the UK to be in breach

---

[19] European Court of Human Rights, 2021, *Lacatus* v *Switzerland* 14065/15, https://hudoc.echr.coe.int/eng#{%22itemid%22:[%22002-13093%22]}

[20] United Nations, 1948, Article 22.

[21] UN, 2006, Convention on the Rights of Persons with Disabilities; UN, 1989, Convention on the Rights of the Child; UN, 2007, Declaration on the Rights of Indigenous Peoples.

[22] UN Human Rights Council, 2012, *Guiding principles on extreme poverty and human rights.*

of human rights. According to a submission by solicitors Mishcon de Reya, human rights legislation was cited in 538 legal cases since the year 2000; in only thirty-nine of those cases, the court made a Declaration of Incompatibility, and eight of those were overturned on appeal. So in total, there have been only thirty-one cases in twenty years where the courts actually declared there was a breach of human rights. The main recurring issues have concerned immigration rights and mental health.[23]

Protection from injustice

It should be clear enough, from what I have said up to this point, that I do not believe that an approach focussed on equalities and human rights is capable of addressing general issues of inequality. The terms in which equalities are framed do not address most of the inequalities that people face; the construction of human rights is minimal. Even taken together, these principles are not enough to defend citizenship for people who have been denied it, or to protect people from social exclusion. However, what this approach has done is different, and positive, and it can be defended in other terms. The central focus of the approach is not the pursuit of equality, or the protection of rights; it is to offer a range of protections to people who would otherwise suffer injustice.

The central principle governing relationships between the welfare state and citizens is the 'rule of law': everyone, including governments, public agencies, corporations and private individuals, is subject to the rules. The best protection for asylum seekers, for example – people who do not have the rights of citizenship – is adherence to a complex system of rules – and conversely, the greatest threat to such people is the willingness of government to ignore them. Where there are no rules, there is 'discretion'; but discretion is dangerous if left without a shape, and it has long been the practice in British government to fetter discretion with a system of administrative rules, intended to protect people from arbitrary power.

In the context of public services, the decision as to whether an action is 'lawful' is generally taken in terms of the 'judicial review of administrative action', or 'judicial review' for short. When the courts are asked to intervene, their first point of reference is the law that is relevant in the particular circumstances – a statute, a statutory instrument (the main source of rules in social security), and the precedent of previous legal judgments. (Academic lawyers are often reluctant to accept statutory provisions at face value; what matters is whether the principle has been tested in a court.) That will usually be sufficient to determine what the rules are, but the courts subject such

---

[23] Mishcon de Reya, 2021, *IHRAR's call for evidence*, https://www.mishcon.com/news/ihrars-call-for-evidence-mishcon-de-reya-response

rules to other criteria, too. Three examples are of particular interest. One is the centuries-old principle of 'natural justice': judges must be unbiased, and people are entitled to a hearing. In my view, current law and practice relating to social security are open to challenge on those grounds. The effect of rules relating to 'mandatory reconsideration' mean that the DWP gets to make judgments about its own conduct, and that claimants with grounds for review are denied a hearing or access to justice until they have been through the procedure. The imposition of sanctions, which can leave people with no resources for months or years, is done without a hearing.

Next, there is the principle of 'promissory estoppel': an official's word binds the agency, and citizens are entitled to redress if wrongful advice or a mistaken judgment leads them to act in ways that make them suffer harm. It used to be the case that overpayments in social security were not recoverable if the agency had made a mistake, and the recipient could not have been expected to know the benefit was wrong – that is no longer true, but it should be.

A third example is the 'Wednesbury' test of reasonableness; if a rule is manifestly irrational, the courts can strike it down. There was a recent example relating to Universal Credit, now the main benefit for people of working age on low incomes. Universal Credit is a horrendous mess, but the rule that was struck down was a very small part of the process: the calculation of what income people in low-paid employment had received in a month. Banks do not operate on bank holidays and weekends, and the Universal Credit assessment ignores that. That has meant, for people unlucky enough to have an assessment marked down for an awkward date, that regular income will be counted as too high, or too low, and the amount they receive will fluctuate wildly. The court was not impressed by the DWP's arguments that changing the assessment in this case would be expensive or inconvenient. The judgment concluded: 'The Secretary of State for Work and Pensions' refusal to put in place a solution to this very specific problem is so irrational that I have concluded that ... no reasonable SSWP would have struck the balance in that way.'[24]

There are major limitations in using the courts, and institutional conventions that make it difficult to obtain their protection. One is the requirement, for judicial review, that all other sources of redress must first have been exhausted – that makes it possible for agencies such as the DWP to kick the ball into touch, deferring action to a point where it will not do the appellant any good. Another barrier is the general requirement for someone protesting the rule to have 'locus standi' as a litigant, to show that they are personally affected by the operation of the rule. It is not usually possible for a charity or public interest defender to challenge a rule that

---

[24] https://www.bailii.org/ew/cases/EWCA/Civ/2020/778.html

is manifestly irrational or unjust, before it hurts people: they have to find someone who has actually been harmed in order to take the case. And then there is the frankly outrageous 'anti-test case' rule: if the DWP has been found to be acting illegally, it does not have to set things right for anyone who suffered before the decision was made.[25] (There are current proposals to extend that principle in other branches of administrative law.[26])

The processes in British law are arcane and often inaccessible, in my view unreasonably so: some of the worst legal breaches affect people who are poor or vulnerable, such as benefit claimants and asylum seekers. This next statement is from a (rather unusual) legal judgment in the Upper Tribunal, against HMRC, the tax authority. The judge's tone is, to say the least, exasperated.

> Well, here we go yet again. I used the phrase 'Well, here we go again' with a sense of frustration, bordering on despair, to open my decision in NI v HMRC [2015] UKUT 160 (AAC), a case in which I criticised Her Majesty Revenue and Customs (HMRC) for both its decision-making processes and its conduct of appeals in relation to tax credits claims. ... So, yes, in short this is yet another sorry tale of HMRC institutional incompetence and inefficiency which could well have led to injustice, were it not for the persistence of the Appellant.[27]

Judicial review – which can only be granted when other measures have been explored and failed – is simply too slow to protect people with limited resources. There have been rapid, urgent actions taken on behalf of some people – such as migrants facing illegal deportation; but there is no obvious equivalent for people who have been left without money for food this week. For most people, there is no effective way of getting legal redress before the penalty, and the problems, have been suffered.

Legal action is costly, too, and the limited funds that have been available for legal aid have become increasingly restricted in recent years. Contingency fees – where lawyers take a substantial proportion of any compensation – have made some kinds of action possible, but in cases where the financial damage is limited, that is not much help. The damage caused by denying someone benefits for six months might amount to less than £2000 – devastating for the person concerned, but hardly enough for a reasonable

[25] *CAO and another* v *Bate*, [1996] 2 All ER 790 (HL).

[26] M Elliott, 2021, *Judicial review reform 1: nullity, remedies and constitutional gaslighting*, https://publiclawforeveryone.com/2021/04/06/judicial-review-reform-i-nullity-remedies-and-constitutional-gaslighting/

[27] *VO* v *HMRC* (TC) [2017], http://www.bailii.org/uk/cases/UKUT/AAC/2017/343.pdf

proportion to meet legal costs. Legal cases have come to depend on support from charities, law centres and public interest actions.

The law relating to equalities and human rights has placed a duty on public agencies to comply with basic principles, requiring the agency to consider how this affects their practice, and appointing a regulator to ensure that those principles are observed. Redress and specific action both depend heavily on access to justice, but that access needs radical improvement. If beyond that we can develop more effective legal protections – a framework to permit rapid redress, public interest actions and judicial restraint of unlawful conduct – it would help to build a system which is more open, more meaningful to people who are disadvantaged, and fairer.

Equalities and human rights

Key points	'Equality' is about the removal of disadvantage. 'Equalities' refer to specific disadvantages.
	The disadvantages can be cumulative.
Positive developments	The services described here, and the principles on which they are founded, were hardly thought of at the time of the foundation of the welfare state.
Where policy has gone wrong	Human rights outline the bare minimum; citizens need more than that.
What to do instead	Legal redress is fundamental to justice, but it only goes so far. The law has to be clearly stated, and legal protection has to be accessible and affordable.

10

The public services

Conventionally, the discussion of the welfare state has focussed on the 'Five Giants' – want, idleness, ignorance, squalor and disease – and the services intended to deal with them. However, the focus of this book has been a discussion of the role of the institutions of the welfare state, rather than a focus on poverty and disadvantage, and the discussion of those institutions would not be complete without a discussion of the public services.

The 'public services' take into account such broad areas as policing, justice, roads, street lighting, waste disposal, museums, libraries and public transport. Public and social services have important elements in common. Many of these services grew from similar roots – in particular, the structures developed to manage the Poor Law, which led to the establishment of local government in the course of the nineteenth century. Social and public services have a definable institutional structure, they are all seen as part of the remit of government, and in so far as they are actually provided directly by government, they are publicly financed. The public services have not, however, always been seen as part of the 'welfare state' – and it is noteworthy that while people who use services such as schools or medical care are being described as 'dependent', people who ask the police for help, walk on a pavement or visit a museum are not. Many of us might wish that social services were viewed more like public services – that the service should there for everyone, and taken for granted in the same way as street lighting or drains – but the fact is that they are not seen as equivalent.

Public services have four key features. The first is that they are services to the public – not in the economic sense, which hinges on what they are selling, but in the social sense, that they actually do something directly to benefit people. Roads, sewers, parks, schools and social housing all deliver services to the public. Public functions which serve government, like IT or audit, do not, so they are not 'public services' in this sense; nor are areas of government activity, however important, which are focussed on other issues, such as economic management or foreign policy.

Second, services are delivered according to public policy, rather than being set up to meet commercial criteria. It is true of the public services, as it is of the social services, that the term encompasses a wide range of activity that is not organised or delivered by the state. Lifeboats, mountain rescue, community centres and voluntary sector libraries are all public services. What makes a service 'public' is not a matter of ownership or control, but its purpose.

Third, public services are redistributive, in the sense that those who pay are not necessarily those who benefit. The pattern of redistribution is not necessarily egalitarian, but when people pay, they should know that their payment is not an individual purchase, and that it will be used to benefit others. Some public services are based on pooled contributions and benefits; some are funded by taxation; in some cases the individual beneficiaries cannot be identified.

These three elements – service, policy and redistribution – lead to the fourth. Public services are operated as a trust. The characteristic operation of a trust is an arrangement where person A (the founder of the trust) pays person B (the trustee) in order to benefit person C (the beneficiary). This kind of arrangement is common in public and social services: schools, hospitals, care homes and prisons are all marked by arrangements where those who pay are not necessarily those who receive, and there is a disconnection between purchase and consumption. In economic terms, the consumer or service user is not the purchaser of services; and the trustee is not an agent of a principal, but operates within a distinct and explicit framework of rules.

There has been a general presumption in political discourse that markets do things better, that private enterprise has an expertise that public services cannot match, and that competition leads to better provision. The preference for commercial services over public provision reflects a somewhat blinkered economic perspective. Markets, the argument goes, are outstandingly good at delivering what people want. However, markets might, on rare occasions, fail, and it is only when they do fail that there is a clear justification for government to act. The Treasury Green Book, used to guide the evaluation of state actions, acknowledges that there are values 'that economic markets are either unable to fully capture, or are unable to register at all. The various forms of shortfall in market welfare optimisation are characterised as "market failures"'.[1]

The main examples of market failure in economics textbooks relate to a wide-ranging, but still limited, set of circumstances.

- *Social goods* are goods which are not divisible or excludable: that is to say, people can use them at the same time as other people. Examples are clean air, roads, parks, policing and public order.
- *Externalities* occur wherever the people who are engaged in market transactions affect the interests of other people who are not party to their decisions. Education is not only important for people who give and receive it; it matters for the preparation of a future workforce, and so affects the whole economy. Health services are not only concerned with people who are ill; their illness can directly affect the position of others.

---

[1] HM Treasury, 2018, *The Green Book*, pp 28–9.

- *Information failure* means that the mechanisms which markets rely on – price stability, informed choice or the absence of monopolies – cannot work. In the context of social care, the Competition and Markets Authority has raised a number of concerns about the operation of the market. Information is poor, and choice is not often exercised. There are inadequate processes for dealing with grievances. And there is a frequent failure, on the part of private providers, to meet legal requirements about prices, costs and charges.[2]
- *Failures of competition.* There are situations where sellers or buyers have an unfair advantage. There may be local monopolies, high entry costs, price fixing and other kinds of barrier to overcome. Many privatised services have been captured by large-scale firms which are particularly adept at applying for government contracts; small, independent contractors cannot compete.

From the point of view of welfare provision, however, market failure in the economic sense is not the biggest problem. Markets are simply not set up to do what public services do. The heart of the issue rests on the idea of 'efficiency'. If markets are operating in the way that economic theorists propose, independent producers will be best able to maximise their returns by reducing the cost of production for each unit of output. Their incentive to do this lies in competition; if competitors can produce the same items more cheaply, they will be able to supply the goods at a lower price. They can reduce the costs of each unit by choosing how much to produce. If some tasks are too expensive, they will be more efficient if they do not do those things. Public services, by contrast, are there mainly to serve the objectives of policy – that is what is 'public' about them. They are effective if they do what they are intended to do, and 'cost effective' if they do it at the lowest possible cost. Cost-effectiveness is quite different from efficiency. The crucial difference between private and public provision of services is this: efficient production is selective. Markets depend on people making choices. Private providers get to choose what they are going to do. That means some people will be left out. Public services, by contrast, do not get to choose what they are going to do. If, for example, they are supposed to provide a universal mail service, delivering to everyone's home, they do not have the option to leave out people who live too remotely to bother with. If they are trying to ensure that everyone has access to a doctor, they cannot refuse to provide for patients who are too sick, or who need treatments that are too expensive. So it is probably going to be true that the private sector can do things more cheaply than the public services. They do that by making choices – either by limiting the scope of what they do, or by

---

[2] B Hudson, 2019, Commissioning for change, *Critical Social Policy*, 39(3), pp 413–33.

excluding people, a process sometimes called 'adverse selection'.[3] And that means, because public services are usually the provider of last resort, that where the private sector has declined to take on services that are isolated, difficult or expensive, it is the public services that are left with the residue.

Public and social services are not much like the economic model of a 'business'. The standard economic models – based on self-interested behaviour, the relationship between principal and agent, or the interaction of producers and consumers – do not apply. Superimposing market-based criteria on the operation of public trusts often leads, not to better or more efficient delivery, but only to patterns of delivery that are different – and so, to outcomes that are not consistent either with individual preferences or with social ones. In the process, both the characteristic values and the benefits of public services can be lost – the development of a public sphere, the creation of social capital, the process of redistribution and the sense of common responsibility.

Universal public services

The welfare state is supposed to ensure 'that all citizens without distinction of status or class are offered the best standards available in relation to a certain agreed range of social services'.[4] In this context, the distinction between public and social services is unimportant – the objective for social services (such as health care or education) is to make them as unexceptionable as public services are (like sanitation or the police service). Universality is one of the key methods for delivering social services on this basis. A universal pension (such as the pension for people over 80 in the UK) is for everyone above a certain age. Universal maternity services are (obviously enough) services for everyone who is pregnant or has a new-born child. Universal primary education is education for every child. Universal education is compulsory because otherwise, some children will be denied it. There are, of course, some places in the world where schooling is not universal and compulsory, and it is fairly clear what the problems are: children get left out because they are poor, because their parents need them to work, and because they are girls.[5]

The distinction between universal and selective services is not so much a matter of the client groups that are served, as of the methods that are used to access the service. Services are universal when they are free at the point

[3] N Barr, 2012, *The economics of the welfare state*, Oxford: Oxford University Press.

[4] A Briggs, 1961, The welfare state in historical perspective, *European Journal of Sociology*, 2(2), pp 228–30.

[5] Unicef, 2018, *Primary education*, https://data.unicef.org/topic/education/primary-education/

of delivery, offered without a test of means or need. The terms of that description are closer to the ideal than to the reality, and it might be helpful to start with a few examples of how universality is understood.

Services for everyone

In the first place, there are public services which provide for everyone. They are there for each and every person, and in principle no one is left out. I have previously discussed two of the key social services that are universal in this sense – education and health care. Here are some further examples.

Public health. The words 'public health' tend immediately to imply a link with health care, but the fields of operation are rather different. Public health extends to the regulation of the environment, the management of food quality, air, noise, housing and sanitation. There are some other reasons for enforcement and monitoring of such standards (such as animal welfare and the regulation of trade) but public health is a basic part of the protection that every person receives. The current COVID-19 crisis only serves to underline its importance.

The rationale for universal, rather than individualised, public health care is straightforward – these are issues that genuinely do affect everyone. It is not up to individuals to decide, as a matter of choice and education, whether or not they can reasonably take the risk of infecting others with a deadly disease; that is a way to kill people.

Police. Policing is there for everyone; in principle, it provides personal security for everyone, and it does not charge the individuals affected for the service. There are some reservations to make about that. First, some other kinds of policing are not there for everyone. There are such things as private security forces, which protect the interests of particular groups, such as residents of particular developments or businesses. Public police forces are sometimes paid to cover public events, such as football matches; in that context, they act as private security might. Second, some police forces are seen as partisan; one of the consistent concerns expressed by poor people around the world is that they feel discriminated against by the police, and the police are not there for them when they are the victims of crime.[6] Neither of those reservations, however, undermines the basic argument. Police are there for public protection; they may sometimes fail in that role, as health services or education may sometimes fail, but it does not mean that they are not there for everyone.

---

[6] D Narayan, R Chambers, M Shah, P Petesch, 2000, *Voices of the poor: crying out for change*, New York: World Bank, pp 162ff.

Fire and rescue services. Fire services are combined with police services in some jurisdictions, because they have something important in common: both are there for public protection. On occasion, too, there are specific issues which elide the distinction between police, fire and rescue – for example, the management of major traffic accidents.

Two of the rescue services deserve special mention. Lifeboats and mountain rescue are universal services that in the UK are substantially (in the case of lifeboats, wholly) within the voluntary sector, rather than government-based. Universality is not equivalent to provision by government.

Services for anyone

There are other are public services which provide things directly and immediately without applying a test, and are subject only to a minimum of conditions. Unlike the first category, they are not literally provided to 'everyone'; they are available to 'all comers' or 'anyone', which is not quite the same thing. But they have in common that they are inclusive and delivered unconditionally, without a test.

Libraries. The development of public libraries is notable as being one of the few areas where universal services did not mainly depend on the actions of government; public libraries were often established through voluntary or philanthropic effort (such as the donations of Andrew Carnegie), and only subsequently absorbed into the system of government. Private lending libraries used to be common, but they have largely disappeared, as have video rental shops; there are other ways of obtaining reading or visual entertainment.

Public libraries are generally available for anyone wishing to use them. They may restrict loans to residents of a local area, but many also have reading space for all comers. (Homeless people may have however been excluded on the basis that the library is not there to provide warmth or bathrooms for all; that is part of a more general problem, applying with equal force to access to shopping malls, doorways and parks.) However, they have suffered greatly during the period of 'austerity', especially in poorer localities, where other services are considered to have a greater priority.[7]

The rationale for making libraries universal is that they offer culture to all, without barriers. (The same rationale applies to museums in the UK,

---

[7] E Davidson, 2020, A new page? The public library in austerity, in J Rees, M Pomati, E Heins (eds) *Social Policy Review 32*, Bristol: Policy Press.

most of which are also available to all comers without charge.) The main controversy about the future of libraries has not been about whether they should be universal, but whether they should continue to exist at all. The internet has become the greatest library in the history of the world, and it has largely taken over from libraries as a source of cultural materials and a resource for research. The defenders of public libraries have pointed to other things that the internet does not provide – access to terminals, a safe environment for children, the provision of a space for study, and an introduction to using books. The debate does however raise the issue that, if there are good cultural reasons for making libraries universal and open, the same arguments apply with no less force to access to the web.

Roads. Roads are available to anyone, but all road users are not equal. The dominance of the motor vehicle has meant that the use of roads by other users, including pedestrians and providing play space for children, has been restricted or eliminated; and motoring is not available to all, but only to those with access to motor vehicles.

The case for universality mainly relates to the idea of roads as public or social goods, which are not excludable – it is not always practical to keep out people who have not paid – and not divisible. There are considerably beneficial externalities from having an adequate road network, because this is basic to communications, labour markets and the delivery of goods and services. However, in this field, as in many others, the argument has been made for charges. Toll roads have been introduced, seeking deliberately to divert non-payers to other routes; congestion and parking charges are used to restrict demand overall, effectively by allowing richer people and commercial users privileged access. These are examples of trying to use pricing as a rationing method, rather than market provision; the conventional models of market provision, by which charges might be related to costs, simply do not work.

Parks. Parks are a further example of social goods, available to anyone. They are excludable – there may be private squares and gardens, restricted to residents with keys – but they are not divisible and they could not exist without some pooling of resources. The argument for accessible 'green' space is that it improves the lives of almost everyone.

Quasi-universal services

Beyond these two categories, there is a large hinterland of services which are not necessarily untested, or free at the point of delivery, and not always unconditional, but which go some part of the way along that path – arguably they could go further. There is a broad range of services to consider.

- *Water*. Charges for domestic water supply used to be incorporated in domestic rates; in Scotland, they are still collected as part of council tax. This implies some (limited) differentiation in charges according to the size and value of the property, but despite the charging structure, the principle is still that the supply of domestic water is inclusive and largely unconditional. There was a period during which people in England would have the domestic water supply disconnected for non-payment, but that has now ceased.
- *Waste disposal*. Domestic waste disposal is charged for in local property taxes, but regular collections are not conditional on payment in most cases and waste has to be cleared regardless; in principle, no one is excluded.
- *Sanitation*. The rules relating to public sanitation are a curious mixture. Many properties have the same arrangements as water supplies, but properties that are not connected to the public sewers have to make their own arrangements.
- *Public toilets*. In England, local authorities were permitted to charge for public conveniences under the 1936 Public Health Act, but not for urinals; that distinction was removed in 2008, on the basis that it discriminated by gender. Some local authorities provide few facilities; some have charges; some make free provision.
- *Public transport*. Public transport typically has some system of paying for fares, but there are subsidies, publicly regulated concessions and in some cases free travel for specified groups.
- *Broadcast media*. There is a flat-rate licence fee for television, but the licence fee has been free for over-75s until very recently (it is now 'passported' to Pension Credit claimants) and radio reception is free for all. Many commercial services are free at the point of delivery.
- *Dentistry and optometry*. Given that the health service is assumed to be universal, the inclusion of these topics in this section may be puzzling – are they not already a universal service? In Scotland dental and optical check-ups are free. In England and Wales, they are subject to charges unless the person is in the long list of exemptions – check-ups are universal for children and older people, free for people in certain identified groups (such as people in prison, pregnant women for dentistry and people with diabetes for optics) and subject to means tests in many other cases. Then there are charges for treatment and for appliances.

These examples lean towards universality, without necessarily fulfilling all the criteria. If they have anything in common, it is that provision is uneven – some things are covered, some are not; and that there is some kind of charge or price built in to the provision. But the same is true, to a lesser degree, of several of the services that are considered clearly 'universal'. The argument for universality is not an argument to make everything public, or unconditional, or to make everything free; it is about making things more public, less conditional, and more nearly free.

The case for universality

Universal services are in most cases provided as a right of citizenship. Citizenship, according to Marshall, is 'a status bestowed on those who are full members of a community. All those who possess the status are equal with respect to the rights and duties with which the status is endowed'.[8] The rights which come into play in discussions of universality are general social rights: general in the sense that they apply to all citizens (unlike personal, particular rights to pensions); social in the sense that they relate to social provision. Too strong an emphasis on the formal structure of rights could however be misleading; the purpose of emphasising universality is to ensure that no one is left out. This is, essentially, an argument about a moral principle.

A second set of arguments is concerned with consequences. If some people are left out, it will affect not just them, but other people besides. The health of the population is affected by the lives and health of the people who live in the same spaces: the measures to stop the spread of COVID-19 are a prime example. Modern economies rely on having an educated, literate workforce; public education is in everyone's interest. More generally, *The spirit level* argues that societies which accept greater inequality also suffer greater crime, poorer health and inferior collective provision.[9]

A third set of arguments is practical. In a time before public fire services, householders used to insure against fire individually, and displayed the sign of the protective service they were subscribed to. Unfortunately, fires do not stop at property boundaries. Water or energy supplies can be individualised – people can buy drinking water in bottles, energy can be generated on the premises – but it makes sense to take advantage of the common route for supply to provide for everyone. A postal service generally works by taking uniform fees from the sender and delivering without charge to the recipient. This is done differently in different countries – some systems make extensive use of *postes restantes*, where people have to go to a central collection point to receive mail. Differentiation and individualisation are possible, but they involve complex, expensive and difficult processes before they can be done. It is simply much easier to establish a common rule.

The practical arguments in favour of universality are often treated dismissively by advocates of economic markets, who hold that it is always better to use the price system for distribution. But when it comes to

---

[8] T H Marshall, 1963, *Sociology at the crossroads*, London: Heinemann, p 87.

[9] R Wilkinson, K Pickett, 2009, *The spirit level*, London: Allen Lane.

practicality, there is an extraordinary example to consider: the case of Google. Google currently provides the world's leading information service – just the sort of thing that universal services are there for. It works across platforms; ownership is not necessary to access or use the service; and it is free at the point of delivery. It is owned and controlled by a multi-national, commercial company, not by government. (The same company, and several other internet services, provide more specialised free services: they include free e-mail services, peer-to-peer communication, free cloud storage, news, library services including access to texts and academic papers, maps and navigation aids.) The pragmatic case for universality is not confined to government activity. Sometimes the process of pricing, testing or selecting recipients is so burdensome that it defeats other objectives (in this case, constructing a bank of saleable data, and finding an audience to advertise to). Sometimes services work better when they do not keep people out. That observation has fuelled arguments for extending universality to a range of services, including communications, transport and legal services.[10]

Although the arguments for universality are shot through with moral concerns, universality is not a principle in itself. It is a method, which can work in some circumstances, but might not work for others. Julian Le Grand has argued that many universal services, including health, education and subsidies to public transport, have effectively served to benefit the better-off.[11] Current arguments for a Universal Basic Income often suffer from the same kinds of distributive impact: the distributive effect of proposals that would replace existing benefits would be to favour those who do not currently receive means-tested social security payments over those who do.[12] Universal provision has advantages for poorer people, who might otherwise be liable to be excluded, but the impact of universal benefits is not necessarily progressive; it depends on what service is being delivered, who receives it, and how it is paid for.

Extending universality

I have considered quite a long list of universal services, but there are other services where related arguments might appropriately be made. Some examples were included as examples of 'quasi-universal' services – there are elements of what they do that already tend towards universality; others are distinctive.

---

[10] Institute for Global Prosperity, 2017, *Universal basic services*, https://www.ucl.ac.uk/bartlett/igp/sites/bartlett/files/universal_basic_services_-_the_institute_for_global_prosperity_.pdf
[11] R Goodin, J Le Grand, 1987, *Not only the poor: the middle classes and the welfare state*, London: Routledge.
[12] P Spicker, 2019, Some reservations about Basic Income, in C Goodman, M Danson (eds) *Exploring Basic Income in Scotland*, Glasgow: Scottish Universities Insight Institute.

Public transport. In Scotland, residents over the age of 60 get a bus pass, granting them free bus travel within the country; there are plans to extend this to young people under the age of 21.[13] The rationale for offering free public transport is not always clear, but a consultation by Transport Scotland offered a range of justifications: countering isolation and loneliness, encouraging older people to get out and about, promoting mobility and independence, helping people to act as carers or volunteers, compensating for low income. Other benefits include promoting a preference for public transport over private, making bus services viable, keeping cars off the road and helping the environment.[14] Some of the submissions to the consultation simply emphasised that this was a benefit that pensioners currently received, and that withdrawing it would make for another cut in their limited income.

There is nothing in these arguments that amounts to an unequivocal justification – this issue is not like the argument for public roads, or libraries, or health care. And yet there are arguments of that kind that can be made. In any argument for universal services, the first step is to argue that there is a legitimate reason to make this the subject of public policy. In this case, there are several. One is that transport is a fundamental 'capability', necessary for people to interact with others.[15] (The term 'capability' comes from Amartya Sen, who argues that capabilities need to be distinguished from the commodities, or different ways of realising the capabilities.) Transport could be provided in lots of ways, but public governance is appropriate because the modes of transport that people use interact with the modes used by other people. The objectives of each person in making a journey may well be individual, but the combined effect of large numbers demands a degree of collective consideration.

The next step is to argue that there should be a service, rather than a market-based solution. The starting point is the incompatibility between market provision and the objectives of public policy. Wherever market criteria apply, producers or providers make choices about the services they are ready to supply. That leads to three phenomena. The first is that profitable routes will be supplied by competing providers – for example, competing for routes that lead between city centres. The second is that unprofitable routes will not be supplied, or will only be supplied at lower frequencies. Those routes in practice tend to be routes to places that

---

[13] Transport Scotland, 2021, *Young person's free bus travel scheme*, https://www.transport.gov. scot/concessionary-travel/young-person-s-free-bus-travel-scheme/

[14] Transport Scotland, 2018, *Consultation on free bus transport for older people and disabled people and modern apprentices*, https://www.transport.gov.scot/consultation/consultation-on-free-bus-travel-for-older-and-disabled-people-and-modern-apprentices/

[15] A Sen, 1999, *Commodities and capabilities*, Oxford: Oxford University Press.

are remote, places which have lower levels of population, places where people have lower disposable income and so are less likely to travel. The third issue is that people who may wish to use the routes supplied in the first case may have no connecting routes supplied in the second. Policy strategists working in this field emphasise the importance of 'integrated transport systems', and one of the main residual roles of public transport has been to shore up feeder routes that are not commercially viable in their own right. Unfortunately, pressures of funding have led to progressive limitation of the range, frequency and coverage of such services.

Once it has been established that there ought to be a service, the next question is whether the service should be universal – extending provision like the pensioner bus pass to other service users. A residual strategy has been tried, and it has failed: the less provision that is made for public transport, the more people are forced to adopt the main other option, which is the motor car. Many rural locations would be unliveable without one. More inclusive strategies that are not universal have been more successful: many European cities have sought to provide effective public transport services at low cost, rather than free, to promote individualist options that are less destructive than the motor car (mainly cycling), and offering a range of alternative forms of integrated transport, including rail, trams and buses. The main objection to this kind of provision is that it is regressive – mainly offering support for the better-off.[16] Transport subsidies reflect the distance travelled, the people travelling the greatest distances most frequently are commuters, who are in work. While the service provided has not been universal, that objection applies to universality with greater force: the principal beneficiaries will be people on relatively higher income. That still leaves the possibility of identifying categories of people who might reasonably be considered as eligible for universal public transport when others are not. The reservations about commuting do not necessarily apply to people who are retired, or to children, and in both those cases the subsidy has a broadly progressive distributive effect – weighted in one part of the distribution by people whose disabilities limit their ability to travel, and in another part of the distribution because of self-selection by people who use cars instead.

Television. Most households in the UK are required to pay for a television licence. The charge for the licence is problematic, because the primary logic of it has little to do with the market or the conventional rationale for charging. The system is a (somewhat unsatisfactory) mechanism for funding the BBC without making it rely directly on a government grant; it is also distributively regressive, taking proportionately more from people on lower

---

[16] J Le Grand, 1982, *The strategy of equality*, London: Allen and Unwin.

incomes than from richer ones, and shamefully punitive, backed by criminal sanctions rather than being treated as a civil debt. The licence fee seems to convey a message that people are paying for a service which they use, but (notoriously) the licence fee is not actually paid for the service that the BBC provides; it is paid for having equipment which has the capacity to receive television signals from any service, which is not at all the same thing, and is probably unsustainable in view of technological advances. There are other ways to fund public broadcasting, such as advertising or linkage with local council tax collection (the same system is used to fund water supplies). Advertising might be insecure; a link to council tax would provide a source of funding that was not directly subject to central government control.

Funerals. There are different ways of managing funerals, and people have hugely diverse preferences about when, how and why different processes should be followed. In the UK, most of this is dealt with through a complex series of exchanges between the families and survivors of the deceased person, and the main way this is managed is through money. Most people who die are older, and many leave property that can be used to meet the funeral expenses. However, others cannot. Currently there are residual arrangements in place to offer a limit amount of assistance with costs. The help available will not meet the cost of a funeral, but only of immediate disposal (usually cremation). Some funerals are managed at public expense, because there is no responsible person to pay for them.

A universal service could meet the costs of cremation or burial, excluding other expenses. This would eliminate one of the main costs of dealing with death. The amount that would need to be spent to make this a universal benefit is very predictable. There is no serious risk of moral hazard – that people will choose to die so as to get a partly subsidised funeral – or of fraud. It might change the balance of decisions to cremate or bury, but burial still comes with substantial expenses – headstones routinely cost more than the burial itself. In the past, cremation has been cheaper, but its expense has been rising, primarily as a result of the need to control emissions and pollution. It would not, however, affect in any way people's ability to make their own arrangements for funerals, or change the relationship with funeral directors. The proposal for a universal support for funeral expenses is only, then, a proposal for a quasi-universal service. The Children's Funeral Fund now does this for dead children – that is, persons who die under the age of 18. Why stop there?

Tuition fees for university students. Student grants were withdrawn when the current system of finance was introduced. They had two main elements: a means-tested maintenance grant, covering living expenses and set against parental income, and support for tuition fees, which were largely free, subject only to the exclusion of parents on very high incomes. The justification for the policy is not strictly financial: it is based in a liberal model of education which argues that everyone should be able to develop in accordance with his or her ability.

Arguably this process was not quite universal, because the basis on which students hold a university place, and are subject to fees, is based on academic selection. Older ('mature') students are not even subject to that. But there is scope for tuition to be made free. If that was done in the same way as secondary education, it might cause difficulties in the management of students from other countries, who have become an increasingly large part of the population of universities; an alternative is the system used in Scotland, where tuition is not formally free, but students receive a nominal grant equivalent to the size of the tuition fee.

The main objection to student grants is that they favour better-off people. The student population is skewed towards the middle classes, and many students go on to become high earners. Neither is a conclusive argument against universality – higher earners pay more in taxation. A secondary objection is that grants are expensive, and as the student population has expanded, the number of grants that would have to be paid increases.

Wi-Fi. The internet is free, and many applications are free, but the apparatus to use it is not. In this case, as in many others, the question of whether the service should be provided is distinct from the question of whether it should be provided to everyone. Before the internet, the French government made Minitel, a computer-like system, available to every household; it was reasoned that it would give the population access to information and commercial services. That intention was undermined by backing the wrong system, but it does not alter the principle.

In relation to the first question, whether a service should be provided, it already is: there is free Wi-Fi in some shops, cafes, trains and buses, and there are other systems that make some bandwidth available, but there are technical solutions to prevent certain types of connection and excessive downloading. (There are also issues relating to encoding and privacy. The importance of privacy can be exaggerated; people are no more in private when they are using a public internet service than they are when they are using a public park, and they are both visible to others and restricted by criminal law.) The principle of access to anyone is already established; it is largely a question of how far that should go. The Labour Party proposed free Wi-Fi during its otherwise disastrous election campaign in 2019.[17]

---

[17] P Walker, R Syal, H Stewart, 2019, Labour's free broadband plan fires up the election battle, https://www.theguardian.com/technology/2019/nov/15/free-broadband-essential-uk-compete-john-mcdonnell-labour-policy-openreach

The impact of broadband on children's education has been highlighted by the experience of the pandemic; there is now an educational and cultural case for extending provision much more widely.

School meals. For much of their history, meals in schools have been available freely only on the basis of a means test. The arrangement was complex, and many children did not receive the provision although they were nominally entitled. This has changed with meals in the first three school years, that is, 'reception' and years 1 and 2. Lower incomes among parents of younger children suggest that the provision is reasonably well targeted.

The case for providing school meals is probably most effectively made by analogy. Universal health care has been taken to include food to patients in hospital. Why is that food not paid for? There are three good reasons. The first is that hospitals get to control and regulate nutrition for patients while they are doing it. Second, price influences choice. If charges are levied, some people will not receive the food; some will opt for alternative expenditure, and bring food in. Both are problematic for effective medical care, and bringing food in adds further problems about hygiene in a controlled environment. Third, the administration required would be complex and burdensome, especially if the charge is geared to the individual items that people do or do not eat. All the same arguments apply to meals in schools. Schools that do not have meal facilities may allow children to go away from school, beyond supervision or direction. Dietary choices ought to be guided, and they are not guided. (Some educational staff report better readiness for learning, concentration, behaviour and progress are improved,[18] but the evidence on those points is not conclusive.) Canteen facilities are frequently inadequate for the numbers of children involved. Things can, and should, be different.

Child care. The arguments for universal child care are hardly new: they have been around at least since the 1970s, when experiments with pre-school provision had shown benefits for children and mothers.[19] There is a clear and direct extension of arguments from universal education – it is simply a question of whether those arguments apply appropriately to children at lower ages, and to children of school age during school holidays.

Universal child care has been developed in several places. France has low-cost child care generally available; Norway introduced a general subsidy for children aged 3–6 in 1975; in 1997 Quebec introduced low-

---

[18] P Sellen, N Huda, 2015, *Evaluation of universal infant free school meals*, Education Policy Institute.

[19] See, for example, A K Williams, 1971, Universal child care, *Young Children*, 26(6), pp 348–54.

cost, regulated child care through subsidies, which has been seen as quasi-universal (though parents have to pay $5 a day, which is still not negligible); Scotland has a policy of developing the equivalent, though there is some way to go. There have been criticisms of the policy: in Quebec, it has been argued that greater participation of women in the labour market has to be offset by lower skills and worse family relationships: 'more access to child care was bad for children and parents in the dimensions captured in our data'.[20] The Norwegian evidence has been neutral over parts of the distribution but does indicate benefits for lower-to-middle income families and possibly some equalisation of outcomes.[21]

This is not, of course, an exhaustive list. It serves to show only that more services could be delivered universally, beyond the constraints of the market. The examples considered here are certainly practical – all have been done, or are being done, to some extent. Bus travel is universal for pensioners. Student tuition fees and TV licences for over-75s used to be paid. Free school meals, some child care and funeral costs are paid for some on a universal basis. In the long list of measures I have been reviewing, only Wi-Fi has not generally been free – but the private sector has been experimenting with universal access in some places. Overcoming any practical obstacles cannot answer the question of whether these things should be done, which is a matter of judgment: priorities, costs and effective methods of delivery have all to be considered.

I think it can reasonably be argued that the more services that are delivered on this basis, the greater will be the basic security offered by the system as a whole. However, universal services cannot all be assumed to act the same way or to be justified in terms of general principles. Their impact has to be identified case by case and service by service.

---

[20] M Baker, J Gruber, K Milligan, 2008, Universal child care, maternal labor supply, and family well-being, *Journal of Political Economy*, 116(4), pp 709–45.
[21] T Havnes, M Mogstad, 2015, Is universal child care leveling the playing field?, *Journal of Public Economics*, 127(C), pp 100–44.

The public services

Key points	Public services are guided by public policy. They work to different criteria from private services.
	Universal services can be available to anyone; some are available to everyone.
Positive developments	At a time when public services have been eroded or privatised, some have gone against the trend: charges for prescriptions and eye tests have been removed in Scotland, charges for museums were introduced but then abolished, several areas have introduced bus passes for older people and those with disabilities, there are planned extensions of free school meals and transport for children.
	Some private firms have recognised the case for free public access.
Where policy has gone wrong	Markets sometimes fail, and market provision is always incomplete. That is tolerable in some fields and not in others.
What to do instead	Some services are better taken out of the private market. The more this can be done, the greater the security the welfare state will offer.

11

Towards a stronger welfare state

In the course of this book, I have spent some time trying to explain that the issues which have captured attention are often a poor guide to the problems or the performance of the welfare state. Because they misrepresent the issues that services have to deal with, they fail to address the problems with those services that people actually experience, and they distract from the things that need to be done.

That is not to underestimate the power of the narrative. If policy-makers are convinced that the welfare state makes people demanding and dependent, that money spent on welfare is wasted, that welfare is being undermined by false and fraudulent claims, that welfare was only ever supposed to be a safety net, they will take action to deal with those supposed problems. In doing that, they often create further problems in turn. Sometimes the problems that leads to are newly minted. People have been plunged into poverty because of the punitive conditionality introduced after 2008; hundreds of thousands of people have had their only source of income stopped for a month or more. Sometimes the problems that are generated are the very problems that they are supposed to be avoiding. For example, measures to target benefits more precisely are liable to generate wrongful payments. The fraud and error associated with the State Pension is estimated to be 0.1%; but the fraud and error associated with the means-tested Pension Credit appears to be 5%, fifty times greater than the non-means-tested benefit.[1] Pensioners are not generally thought to be fraudulent, and the first figure shows they are not; the second figure shows what goes wrong when the criteria become more detailed. Tighter controls lead to stricter boundaries, and stricter boundaries lead to problems in policing those boundaries.

Some wrong directions

In just about every area of policy I have considered, policies have been diverted, deflected or misplaced because of a set of misconceived beliefs. Four of the false trails stand out as particularly destructive.

---

[1] DWP, 2016, *Fraud and error in the benefit system*, https://www.gov.uk/government/uploads/system/uploads/attachment_data/file/528719/fraud-and-error-prelim-estimates-2015-16.pdf

Choice and personalisation

'Personalisation' has been argued for in a wide range of services – including services to older people, psychiatric patients, learning disability, people with addictions, offenders, school pupils, homeless people, benefit recipients and the unemployed. The central premise is that people should have a choice about the service they receive.

Choice means lots of things in public policy. In education, it seems to be about diversity; in health care, about responsiveness to users; in social housing, about personal responsibility and control.[2] A choice implies, Dan-Cohen argues, some kind of selection, choosing to do some things and not to do others; and opportunity costs, because people have to accept that some choices are set aside in order to select others.[3] Choice does not mean that people get what they want; it means only that they get to decide.

The arguments for personalisation are well-meaning. They are based in a critique of the existing forms of provision, and a belief that greater choice and control can counter present deficiencies.

> The current system has long come under criticism for its top-down approach to service planning and provision with little say for service users over the services they receive and how they receive them. Personalisation is proposed as a means to move away from a one-size-fits-all approach towards provision which meets the individual needs and requirements of users.[4]

This can be seen as an attempt to extend the choice and diversity associated with markets to situations where the market does not operate. The very fact that the market does not operate, however, points to the flaws inherent in the model. Personalisation is being introduced in circumstances where access and distribution are not otherwise offered by commercial providers – that is why it has to be done within the framework of social services, rather than being left to people to arrange from their income.

Personalisation is very similar in form to the arguments that have been made for markets in the provision of welfare – the link with individual budgeting is not coincidental. Reform, a think tank, has argued for a massive extension of personal budgets into fields including education, health, employment services and criminal justice: 'placing money into the hands of

---

[2] I Greener, M Powell, 2009, The evolution of choice policies in UK housing, education and health policy, *Journal of Social Policy*, 38(1), pp 63–82.

[3] M Dan-Cohen, 2002, *Harmful thoughts*, Princeton: Princeton University Press, p 126.

[4] J Harlock, 2009, *Personalisation: rhetoric to reality*, London: National Council for Voluntary Organisations, p 4.

individuals to acquire their own public services'.[5] While I think there is a strong case for people to have money for the things they buy in the market, such as food, in general terms I have been arguing for the opposite – taking more services out of the market, or 'decommodification'. There are three main objections to personalisation in principle. The first is the assumption that needs are best met through the exercise of choice between a range of options. That depends on circumstances. Individual choice requires the individual to make the decision. People may not be free to make choices, or lack the capacity to do it: for example, people unable to return home from a hospital bed are seriously limited in their ability to examine the options. Choice relies on there being a range of options; the choices may not be available, and the more complex, unusual or difficult a person's circumstance, the less likely it is that eligible choices will be available.

The second key objection lies in the idea that needs are best met on an individual basis. There are circumstances where that is true, but there are also many circumstances where it is not. Some services are best delivered generally, such as roads and water supplies; some are delivered universally, such as health insurance and pensions; others may be delivered to groups of people, such as schooling. Against the model of personalisation, we should set the case for mass provision. It might not be as appealing as a personalised response, but it is a lot more practical. If – as I have argued – we need houses, care workers, care homes, community hospitals and basic benefits, those things require a mass programme, and a highly individualised, fine-tuned response is no way to go about it.

The third objection, of course, is that markets do some things rather badly. I discussed the issues in the previous chapter, but there is more to say.

Privatisation and marketisation

Privatisation is a blunt-edged term. It might mean that services are shifted into the profit-making private sector; it might mean that services are subject to the disciplines of the market; it might just mean that the services are financed in a way that takes them off the government's books. The biggest contractors for public work make their profits, not by providing services themselves, but by a co-ordinated and complex programme of sub-contracting which mobilises the resources of many smaller suppliers.

Probably the most frequently voiced objection to the private sector is that it is extractive: it makes profits out of providing services, which otherwise could be used for the public benefit. It does happen that some suppliers are extractive – the residential care sector is increasingly dominated by a

---

[5] C Martinez, J Pritchard, 2019, *Proceed with caution*, London: Reform.

model designed to divert returns into profits abroad.[6] However, profits are not intrinsically objectionable. If a local authority wants to purchase office furniture, it does not do that by going into furniture production; it buys it from a supplier, who will make a profit on the deal.

The difficulty here is that the sort of activities being undertaken by public agencies are not, for the most part, like buying furniture. The nature of a personal 'service', Steven Osborne argues, is that it is done for a person or group of people, and that they have to be there, taking part, for the service to be delivered.[7] There are some services that can be separated from the recipient, such as financial and legal services; and there are other services which can be supplied by different people for a limited time, like hairdressing or taxi rides; but most public services are not like this. The prime objection to the involvement of the private sector and business principles is not that they introduce charging mechanisms, or that they do not work, or even (as sometimes happens) that they do not necessarily know what they are doing; it is that their involvement changes the character of the service provided.

'Marketisation' depends on a sort of translation, where services can be configured as commodities and dealt with by market principles. That has two stages. The first is commodification – identifying what is a unit of service, which can be priced. There are some public services where there is no great difficulty in deciding about that. For a mail service, it is getting a letter or parcel delivered; for a refuse collection service, it is emptying a bin and taking the refuse to be disposed of. However, when it comes to other services – care for older people, probation, support into employment – it is a little less obvious what the unit of output is, or ought to be. This has been a recurring problem in the privatisation of employment support – it is not as easy as saying that someone has got a job. Contracting firms have to show that they have made a lasting difference; they were not able to do that adequately within the constraints of the Work Programme, and that is why that programme failed.

The second stage is commoditisation, a process I discussed in the context of social care. If there is going to be any competition, the units provided by different competitors have to be standardised to some degree; they have to be comparable (so that purchasers can determine which is better value) and substitutable (so that purchasers can make a meaningful choice between them). Commoditisation makes sense in any competitive market. There can be some distinctions between products, but commoditisation is why cars have their controls in familiar places, why computers run with

[6] D Burns, L Cowie, J Earle, P Folkman, J Froud , P Hyde, S Johal, I Rees Jones, A Killett, K Williams, 2016, *Where does the money go?*, Manchester: CRESC.

[7] S Osborne, Z Radnor, G Nasi, 2013, A new theory for public service management?, *American Review of Public Administration*, 43(2), pp 135–58.

standard operating systems and why light bulbs have standard fittings. The reason why so many councils have switched to wheelie bins is not because there are not different ways of managing rubbish collections; it is because rubbish collection has become commoditised, as a standard, substitutable product. And, in the case of social care, standardising the level of care, the support that is offered and the time periods for which care is allowed reflects the same kind of thinking. Private residential care, the CRESC report argues, is increasingly based on the model of a Travelodge. 'An unintended consequence of the chain business model is a future in which care homes are increasingly alike. By default, society must then accommodate its older people in large, full service hotels of single rooms with en-suite, in a setting which is more institutional than domestic.'[8] Similarly, treating domiciliary help as a series of 15-minute packages of time has made it possible for firms behave as if they were letting out hotel rooms. However, the approach also has the effect that people can be faced with a bewildering series of care workers coming through their doors.

Much of the impetus behind marketisation has been a general belief, reinforced by some pretty dodgy economic theory,[9] that private businesses and markets simply do things better than public services. This, as I have explained, stems from a misunderstanding. Public services and private businesses do things differently; they are meant to. The services operate in different ways, on different criteria. Markets leave gaps, necessarily. The advocates of free markets are always eager to remind us that people have a choice. So do the producers – it is absolutely fundamental to the idea of the free market that they must. There are circumstances where markets do not work well, and cases where they do not work at all. And wherever this applies, the public services are left to pick up the pieces.

Individualisation: the atomised society

Underlying arguments for both privatisation and personalisation there is a deeper philosophical stance: that what matters is the decision of each individual, and that individuals should be able to exercise choices, making all the decisions about the things that affect them. Hayek, one of the leading thinkers of the radical right, argued:

the presumption that each man knows his interests best ... is neither plausible nor necessary for the individualist's conclusions. The true basis of his argument is that nobody can know *who* knows best and that

---

[8] Burns et al, 2016, p 10.
[9] For example, R Starr, 1997, *General equilibrium theory*, Cambridge: Cambridge University Press; and see my critique in P Spicker, 2013, *Reclaiming individualism*, Bristol: Policy Press.

the only way by which we can find out is through a social process in which everybody is allowed to try and see what he can do.[10]

This is expressed in the elevation of individual choice, a mistrust of the judgments of professionals or state agencies; and distribution through market mechanisms. Dowding points to a series of issues where governments have opted to interpret social problems in terms of individual choice and action: his examples include the management of obesity, gambling, drug use and housing provision (which has increasingly been left to the private market).[11] We can add to that list much that is done in the field of public health – smoking, alcohol abuse, decisions about vaccination and arguments against lockdown during the control of COVID-19. Individualism is often taken to imply a degree of 'atomisation' – a situation where everyone is seen either as an individual, or part of a narrowly defined 'bubble', such as a family or a household, a denial that a 'society' has any meaning, and a general view that actions taken by the state are illegitimate.

Individualism does not have to be taken this way. Rational individuals collaborate. There is nothing in the assertion of freedom, rights and human dignity that is not compatible with the idea of the welfare state.[12]

There is a common thread running between this position and the topics discussed before it. All of them reflect the priorities of 'neoliberals'. That term covers a range of views, but there are two key elements: a stance that personal freedom depends on individuals making decisions without the intervention of the state, and a belief that distribution through a competitive economic market is the best way to ensure that people's welfare is enhanced. Neoliberalism is an idealistic moral position, but it also appeals directly to individual self-interest, and is reinforced by the advantages it offers to those with propertied interests. It should not be assumed, however, that those interests are the only factors that have influenced the trend to individualisation. Arguments for personalisation, choice and control by service users are often made by those on the political left. People from across the political spectrum can hold to bad ideas for good motives, but that is not enough to turn them into good ideas.

Addressing common problems

There are genuine problems in the British welfare state. They are just not much like the problems which are identified in the criticisms of the radical right.

---

[10] F Hayek, 1948, *Individualism and economic order*, Chicago: University of Chicago Press, p 15.

[11] K Dowding, 2020, *It's the government, stupid*, Bristol: Bristol University Press.

[12] Spicker, 2013.

The problem of size. The promise that the welfare state held out was not that it would be comprehensive: it was that it would proceed by 'ensuring that all citizens without distinction of status or class are offered the best standards available in relation to a certain agreed range of social services'.[13] The problem of size is rooted in the very nature of the 'welfare state' – with what it is trying to do. The key issue I want to raise here is not the range of social services, though that has been the subject of much of this book; it is the problem inherent in providing any major public service inclusively and extensively. The welfare state, from the outset, had a mass role. It was intended to deal, and did deal, with vast numbers of people – health cover for the whole population, free (secondary) schooling for millions of children, hundreds of thousands of new homes every year – building to a peak of six million council houses. Major activities have to be funded, land has to be available to build on, resources and expertise have to be marshalled, trained staff have to be employed. The sheer size of the operation had, and has, implications for how things are done.

Responding to individual circumstances. Another manifestation of the problem of size has implications for the management of individualised responses. The process of individualised assessment and response calls for huge amounts of data about the individuals in question. Further, preserving equity between service users calls for an extensive set of rules, so that the assessments and responses can be guided by consistent principles. This is annoying and massively intrusive, but it implies something else, too; it assumes that governments have the capacity to manage issues this way.

This is a mistake that governments have made repeatedly. Selective services are touted as being efficient, effective and prudent. That sounds as if it ought to be true, but in practice selectivity is difficult and expensive to manage. There are problems of equity, particularly at the borderlines, and problems when benefits and services are withdrawn. There are mistakes, which run into billions of pounds – the mistaken exclusion of some, and the mistaken inclusion of others. There are problems of take-up: selective services consistently fail to reach a substantial proportion of the people entitled to them. (Atkinson points out that this is not the same as saying that they do not reach the right people: it can happen that the rules only approximate the target groups, and that there is a process of self-selection which holds demand in check.[14] It might be true, for example, that people don't claim Pension Credit because they know that there are things in

---

[13] A Briggs, 1961, The welfare state in historical perspective, *European Journal of Sociology*, 2(2), pp 228–30.

[14] A B Atkinson, 1989, The takeup of social security benefits, in *Poverty and social security*, Brighton: Wheatsheaf.

their personal affairs, such as capital holdings, that would block them from receiving it. However, take-up is still poorly understood; it is just as likely, if not more so, that the people who fail to claim will be the ones that the government most wanted to reach.)

The most egregious example of administrative overconfidence at present – or arrogance, if you prefer the word – is Universal Credit. Universal Credit is intended to deal with seven to eight million people – that in itself should be a warning that anything that was proposed would be difficult to achieve. Universal Credit is designed on the principle that it should be possible, using modern technology, to respond in 'real time' to changes in individual circumstances. The benefit has lurched and stumbled through a long series of failures: the 'reset' after initial attempts to digitise the information failed, criticisms for high levels of fraud and error, the failure of attempts to share real-time information with HMRC, condemnation by the Court of Appeal for inflexibility that was held to be irrational and unlawful,[15] parliamentary concern about the extended waiting time before the first payment, and so on. Much of the blame has been attached to the computer programmes, which could not cope with issues such as verification, non-banking days, or the mass applications that swamped the system with the arrival of COVID-19; but the reality is more troubling. No technology, no matter how sophisticated, can go faster than the information that is fed into it. People do not always know if they are in paid employment, a stable partnership; they often cannot tell whether they are disabled. We are trying, Richard Titmuss argued more than fifty years ago, to set technology to resolve the complexities of human life that we don't know how to deal with at present.[16] That argument is still good today.

There is a general principle here. Governments may want to know more about people's needs and circumstances, and to try to ensure that services really focus on the right people. On occasions, they may have formed the idea that the data they are collecting can be used for planning (one of the justifications for social care assessments), to monitor standards (school tests), to improve service quality (performance indicators in health) and to inform the public; it is debatable whether any of those works quite as intended, but the arguments are not unreasonable. This may all be done for the best of motives. The basic problem is that governments ask for too much – more than they can manage, more than people can really tell them, and more than they really need for effective policy. They over-reach themselves.

Centralisation. The welfare state in Britain has been a powerfully centralising force, and it would be misleading to gloss over that uncomfortable fact.

---

[15] https://www.bailii.org/ew/cases/EWCA/Civ/2020/778.html

[16] R Titmuss, 1968, Universal and selective social services, in *Commitment to welfare*, London: Allen and Unwin.

Politicians tend to have high expectations of the agencies they rely on: they seem to think that if they show 'leadership' and a policy goes in at the top, the outcome they expect to deliver will come out at the bottom. When that does not happen – it would be extraordinary if it did – it becomes fuel for the argument, not to make more realistic policies, not to delegate more effectively, but to tighten central control. The trend has been evident in health services, where currently the government is proposing to restore direction to the Secretary of State; in education, where there is a national curriculum and national testing; in social security, which has been directed from the centre since the Beveridge report; and, of course, in management of the economy, where the Treasury has taken a prominently directive role.

There are some reasonable arguments for a degree of centralisation. One of the key arguments for centralisation is that, in some fields of action, people want and expect there to be a certain uniformity. Common standards in health care, in particular, are seen as a matter of equity and social justice. Variations in educational attainment have been tolerated, but they prompt disquiet, and much of the recent movement to centralisation – including the national curriculum, and the extensive use of testing – has been based in an attempt to reduce the effect of local differences. There are mixed feelings about the uniformity of the benefits system, because there can be marked differences in the cost of living in different areas, mainly attributable to housing, transport and energy costs; but the strength of pleas for a universal basic income rest in large part of the feeling that payments would be fairer if they began from a common, national standard.

None of that, however, really explains the strength of direction from central government. The United Kingdom is a unitary state. Unlike federal governments, which share authority with constituent local or regional governments, the structure of authority in Britain works from the top down. Parliament is sovereign, which means that it is the primary source of legal authority; the devolved governments in Britain can only act within the scope of authority that has been devolved to them, and that authority can be withdrawn at any time. Local authorities in the UK have been gradually stripped of their power. Before 1939, local authorities had been responsible for a wide range of services, including hospitals, energy supply, water, policing, fire services and public assistance; all were removed from them by 1948, with only residual roles on governing committees for some local government representatives. In subsequent years local authorities have largely ceased to be responsible for schools, colleges, public health and, in most places, public housing. They cannot undertake local enterprise, they are not permitted to borrow money or, in most cases, to issue bonds.

Central government has a wide range of controls that can be used to fetter local government. Some controls are legal: the government can direct local authorities on the basis of statute, require local authorities to submit schemes for approval, or make local authority action subject to central consent. They can make the local authority subject to regulation; they can impose an inspectorate or audit procedures; and they can make local authority decisions subject to individual legal action, which happens with planning appeals. There are financial restraints, which many local authorities would consider to be at least as important. This includes not only the direct provision of money, but loan sanction – the power to raise money by borrowing – and systems of financial accountability, in the shape of audit. Then, quite apart from the mandatory controls, there is advice. Central government departments use circulars to advise local authorities how to act. The process of audit, and in particular the identification of good practice in terms of 'best value', has long stretched into specific controls on how local authorities go about their business.

The process of central direction has not always run smoothly. There are obviously political constraints, and there are limits to what can be achieved by passing a law. There is often confusion about which body is responsible for what – for example, the divisions between health and social care – and it has been difficult to organise a co-ordinated policy when advice goes from one central department to only a section of local government. Institutions matter: some reforms take years to be realised.

Co-ordinating services. One of the recurring tropes of the last fifty years has been the complaint that welfare services operate in 'silos'. The division of labour between services had emerged over time, as the services became more complex. One agency, such as a social work department, might have to negotiate relationships with multiple health providers, a range of private firms in social care, and other public agencies such as housing or education services.

There are serious obstacles to co-ordination. Wherever there are defined budgets, there will be the question of who pays for what in specific cases. The agencies, and the professionals, may legitimately have different aims; the recommendation of some reports to over-ride different priorities and collaborate regardless[17] risk undermining professional standards. However, it is very questionable whether the construction of common supervisory agencies, such as Community Planning Partnerships or Integrated Joint Boards, overcomes any of those obstacles. Some partnerships are 'strategic', intended to develop joint responses to identified problems;

---

[17] For example, in C Christie (Chair), 2011, *Christie Commission on the future delivery of public services*, https://www.gov.scot/publications/commission-future-delivery-public-services/; Department of Health and Social Care, 2021, *Integration and innovation: working together to improve health and social care for all*, https://assets.publishing.service.gov.uk/government/uploads/system/uploads/attachment_data/file/960548/integration-and-innovation-working-together-to-improve-health-and-social-care-for-all-web-version.pdf

some are 'communicative', developing networks and providing a forum for discussion.[18] What these bodies can most effectively do is to create relationships, bringing together agencies – such as health and policing – which otherwise would have little insight into each other's approach and priorities. They cannot magically transform the purposes or character of the services they represent.

Services, to be effective, need to have a division of labour, so that everyone knows just what they have to do, and what they should leave to others. The first step, then, is not to pursue greater co-ordination, but its opposite: to ensure that it is always clear where responsibility lies, and that the agency has the capacity and resources to fulfil its role. The most effective way of doing this is to reduce the interaction between services to the greatest extent possible. The more that services can be treated as simple, stand-alone issues, with no effect on other services, the easier they are to manage and to deliver. I have argued in this book for a range of services to be treated separately from others: for example, breaking employment services away from social security, starting to deal with homeless people by arranging housing rather than starting by trying to deal with all their problems, and offering specific universal services to cover a range of issues, such as burial and cremation or Wi-Fi. The main exception to that lies in the construction of the 'care package' for individuals, and the problem there lies in the type of service that is being offered, not that the care package doesn't also supply health care or housing.

The most problematic issues in practice arise at the boundaries, when the services have different concerns and priorities. There are problems, for example, when a hospital wants to discharge an older person, but residential care has to be arranged from a different budget. The barriers will not be resolved just because residential care and hospitals become part of an 'integrated' service – they will still have to be budgeted separately. (The same problems make it difficult enough within the health service to refer people from a general ward to a rehabilitation ward; rehab is expensive.) It is very unclear how the existence of a joint board would make much difference to this situation; 'joining up' services generally means that services are lumped together, not that they become one service with a common purpose. What might make a difference is the existence of dedicated funding for issues that cut across different budgets – the pattern of joint finance, introduced in the 1970s, which made it possible to devote services to groups, such as people with intellectual disabilities, who had previously been under-served. But another way of looking at that is not to suppose that coordination was what was needed; what actually happened was that a specific fund came to be used for a specific category of problems. Wherever there are specific

---

[18] I McDonald, 2005, Theorising partnerships, *Journal of Social Policy*, 34(4), pp 579–600.

problems, it helps to know what can be done. Blurring the lines makes things more difficult.

Managing complexity. There is no point in pretending that complexity does not exist; but the way to deal with complex issues is not to meet them with an equally complicated response. It is to break down the large problem into smaller problems, and if necessary to break down the smaller problems into smaller problems still, until we finish with measures that we can actually do something about. I have made a case for a greater degree of universality. One of the key arguments for universal services is not just that they are simple in their own right; it is that they make the problems which are left more manageable. The health service and free schooling have wiped out some of the principal causes of poverty and debt. A partial basic income, such as the pension or Child Benefit, means that many demands for support – for food, clothing, fuel – no longer have to be made; raising their level would have a substantial impact on the poverty and insecurity that remains. Minimum standards in housing – some of which are now under threat, as the housing market is increasingly deregulated – have cut away many related problems in health and poverty.

It will never be possible to dispense with selectivity and individual assessment altogether, but we could reduce the burden – both to agencies and to service users – by reducing the demands for information. If we subsidise houses rather than personal incomes, we can base it on existing assessments about the property – we do not need to know people's personal details, only that they live there. We do not need to know about every change in sources of income before we can compensate people for unemployment. People are often vague about whether or not they are disabled, but a host of disabling conditions – such as impaired vision, impaired hearing and stroke – could be certified relatively straightforwardly, greatly reducing the complexity of the process of assessment. Whatever governments ask for, it should be minimally intrusive. If they cannot operate a policy under that constraint, they are trying to operate the wrong policy.

Paying for welfare: austerity, retrenchment and reform

At several points in the history of the welfare state, governments have sought to make major cuts in the resources available to it. The period immediately after the war was a time of major financial stringency, with rationing still in place, but the key measures in health, social security, education and housing were introduced regardless. By 1950, the NHS seemed to be in difficulties, and the Labour government introduced a range of charges for services which had been free – prescriptions, optics and dentistry. In the 1970s, also under Labour, there was major retrenchment in the services, and mass closures of hospitals. Then there was the government of Margaret Thatcher, which pledged to 'roll bank the frontiers of the state'. And more recently, there was the 'austerity' imposed by the Coalition government of 2010, and more recently by further Conservative governments.

'Austerity' is something of a misnomer. The welfare state was born during an 'age of austerity';[19] governments had to manage with limited resources, stripping away inessentials, carefully rationing services. The UK NHS was always thought of as an 'austere' service,[20] with much of its attention focused on making the best use of the limited resources it had. Austerity came, in the hands of chancellor George Osborne, to mean something completely different. Philip Alston, the UN Special Rapporteur on Extreme Poverty and Human Rights, observes: 'The driving force behind austerity in the UK has not been economic but rather a commitment to achieving radical social re-engineering – a dramatic restructuring of the relationship between people and the State.'[21] Austerity was taken to reduce the role of the state, to promote privatisation, marketisation and choice. Transferring costs from the public sector to the private market only removes the costs from the public accounts – private goods and services still have to be paid for. And, Alston emphasises, the process may be false economy, generating additional costs as externalities.[22]

I have already discussed some of the key concepts behind retrenchment, but a major element remains to be considered: the relationship of the welfare state to economic policy. In the immediate post-war period, the dominant economic paradigm was Keynesian. The Keynesians argued that the economy had to be seen as a whole, that the economy had to be managed to promote growth and avoid sharp declines in economic activity, and that expenditure on welfare had a major role in ensuring financial stability. The resurgence of classical economics, fuelled by the problem of inflation, led governments to change their emphasis, and economic mechanisms that were originally intended to manage and stabilise growth became a vehicle for the management of cuts. Monetarism argued the key to inflation was to manage the amount of money in the economy, and that public sector spending was a major part of this. Britain's economic problems were caricatured

---

[19] M Sissons, P French (eds), 1963, *The age of austerity 1945–51*, Harmondsworth: Penguin.
[20] For example, J Iglehart, 1983, The British National Health Service under the Conservatives, *New England Journal of Medicine*, 309(20), pp 1264–8; J Carrier, I Kendall, 1998, *Health and the National Health Service*, London: Athlone Press, p 79; I Zweiniger-Bargielowska, 2002, *Austerity in Britain: rationing, controls and consumption 1939–1955*, Oxford: Oxford University Press; G O'Hara, 2007, *From dreams to disillusionment*, Basingstoke: Palgrave Macmillan, p 167.
[21] UN Human Rights Council, 2019, *Report of the Special Rapporteur on extreme poverty and human rights on his visit to the United Kingdom of Great Britain and Northern Ireland*, UN General Assembly A/HRC/41/39/Add.1, p 5.
[22] UN Human Rights Council, 2019, p 5.

as the product of state activity, which was unproductive and a drain on the economy.[23]

In the course of the 1960s and 1970s, the Treasury gradually acquired greater powers. A system initially intended to facilitate managerial efficiency and economic planning became a mechanism for controlling public expenditure, in the belief that this represented sound finance. The Treasury asserted its right to intervene whenever cost implications arose; reserved to itself the control of all budgetary matters, such as tax, national insurance and government borrowing.[24] It treated public sector spending and borrowing as something different in kind from private sector activity.

Cuts in services in the name of 'austerity' have caused serious damage, in two ways. In general economic terms, the effect of withdrawing money from the economy is to reduce the total level of demand, and that leads in turn to a reduction in economic activity. There is a 'multiplier' at work: the effect of whatever the state is doing is magnified. The central fallacy in the strategy of austerity has been the counter-productive belief that governments can cut their way out of a crisis. Within the current structure of the UK economy, it can't be done; the main effect of cuts is to limit future income and revenue. The other main implication has been for the public services. The constant stress on stringency has left services depleted and often unable to cope with changing circumstances. It should not be assumed that all we have to do to correct this is to pay more for the services. If resources continue to be diverted into policies that can never work adequately – such as personalisation, privatisation and marketisation – we must expect to fail.

Many people will consider that the finance poses an insuperable obstacle to reform. The costs of some of the services I have been reviewing are easily justified: the health service is highly cost-effective, primary education is invaluable socially, child protection is mainly there for a relatively small group but is clearly necessary. The extra cost of universalising several of the services I have referred to would be marginal, and much less than the costs governments were willing to pay during the banking crisis or the pandemic. However, the issues I have been raising in this book will not be resolved cheaply, and some other suggestions I have made would call for eye-watering sums of money. Examples are the calls for a massive increase in housebuilding, a major expansion of the scope of public employment, or the wholesale extension of social care. The need for funding is not only very large, not only recurring, but indefinite, in the sense that any major improvement is liable to generate further claims on resources in its turn.

---

[23] R Bacon, W Eltis, 1978, *Britain's economic problem*, London: Macmillan.

[24] N Deakin, R Parry, 1993, Does the Treasury have a social policy?, in N Deakin, R Page (eds) *The costs of welfare*, Aldershot: Avebury.

I do not propose, however, to attach specific costs to proposals at this stage: they could only be provisional, short-lived and open to dispute. It seems more important to identify the limitations of such an exercise. Before a tally of priorities and costs can be constructed, there are some conventions in the way that costs are understood that ought to be challenged. The first concerns the weight that is attached to public spending as opposed to other economic activity. There is a tendency in some circles to treat costs as if they only mattered when they are incurred by governments. Paying for the poorest 20%, the argument goes, has got to be cheaper than paying for everyone. It should be possible to dismiss that argument out of hand. It is only cheaper for government; it leaves the other 80% with the costs of paying for themselves. From the viewpoint of public policy, the total cost, both public and private, is what should matter.

The second convention concerns what is counted. Collective provision outwith the market makes a large – and largely forgotten – contribution to the reduction of poverty. Health and education have been substantially decommodified, or taken out of the market. Their cost is primarily the cost of labour, buildings and equipment. The benefits are rarely considered in discussions of public spending. Every citizen in the UK receives the benefit of comprehensive health insurance, regardless of whether they receive care or not. Nearly every child in the UK of school age has the benefit of schooling. If these were accounted for in terms of their financial value to personal income, they would make a substantial difference to the assessment.

Third, it is often objected that services which are paid for publicly should not affect the position of people who are not using the services. A lot of the apparent cost of the welfare state is down to 'churning' – people are taxed to pay for a service, and then receive the benefits of that service by another route. Churning excites a lot of criticism in the press – why, they say, should rich people get things they don't need? – but then they usually go on to propose arrangements which are vastly more complicated and inefficient, such as means-testing huge numbers of people to decide who should get a bus pass. With income tax, there is only one means-test; with means-tested benefits, there can be fifty or more. (That is not an exaggeration, even if it sounds like one. In 1968, Mike Reddin identified more than 3000 means tests at local authority level, of which more than 1500 had distinctive or unique rules.[25]) The simplest, and most practical way, of delivering public services is to treat them as a collective activity, and to pay for them collectively.

The fourth convention concerns the question of how the cost will be met. If any expansion of welfare provision is to be sustainable, it has to be

---

[25] M Reddin, 1968, Local authority means-tested benefits, in P Townsend (ed) *Social services for all*, London: Fabian Society.

financed in a form which will be accepted – not so much by the public, because overt tax rebellions are rare, as by politicians, who find it difficult to resist the twin temptations, of tweaking the allocation of resources to meet their own priorities, or adding extra rules, qualifications and reliefs to tax regimes. One of the recurring myths of welfare policy is that the finance of any major initiative must depend on income tax. Income tax is important, but it is not by any means the only option open to governments. Other options for taxation might include local sales taxes (as done in the USA), earmarked contributions (the German measure to expand social care provision), occupational levies (the foundation of French pensions), betterment levies (taxing the publicly created value of infrastructure) or a reformed council tax – the present scheme is highly regressive. Beyond taxation, there are many other potential sources of income, such as state enterprise, the sale of licences, and returns on state investment or venture capital. The genius of the Liberal reform in 1911, and later of the Beveridge scheme, was that those schemes built in mechanisms for finance that would make it possible for the system to be self-sustaining; one of the more successful innovations of recent years, the auto-enrolment of workers in occupational pension schemes, has the potential to do as much, so long of course as those funds are fully secured and employers and managers are not permitted to divert the money.

We need to think about public spending differently. I made the case, in the discussion of social security, to recognise that 'transfer payments' are different from government spending. If the transfer is paid for by personal taxation – that is not the only way for governments to raise money – then benefits are simply redistributive. Redistributive transfers should, in principle, have very little impact on the economy – they do not directly affect the money supply, inflation or the overall level of economic activity. If the transfers are not paid for by personal taxation, the economic implications are a little more complex, but it is still possible to view the transfer as more or less neutral in economic terms. (Government finance does not work to a strictly balanced budget, and it is quite possible that some of the money will simply have been created, like 'quantitative easing' or 'helicopter money'. In present circumstances, following the pandemic, there is a very strong argument for government to maintain a flow of money in order to shore up economic demand. Quite apart from that, of course, the case for protecting people on low incomes while that happens is strong in its own right.)

The costs of reform will be high, however the calculations are made. In any reform, too, there will be losers as well as gainers. It is in the nature of almost any reform that shifting resources from one activity to another will benefit some people and make others worse off. Every selective improvement runs the risk of generating new boundaries and new divisions. And wherever services have developed incrementally, as they have done for example in social care, benefits for people with disabilities, social housing or child protection, there will be anomalies and distinctions that seem difficult to justify in hindsight. The way to minimise the losses is to level up provision, and to protect people during transitions: that process will be expensive. There are always choices to be made, and a question to address: whether the money could be used better in another way.

The process of reform

Anthony Crosland made a powerful case against utopian visions. No government, he argued, can transform society instantly by decree. Reform takes time; it is always gradual. The very fact of gradual change, however, implies that any effective reform will change the conditions which led to it being introduced; and, with the passage of time, there will be new issues, and new priorities.[26] Reforms have to be realistic. They have to be robust, in the sense that any new policy has to be capable of adapting to future services. And they have to be capable of responding to problems, and accommodating further change.

Many governments have pursued structural reforms eagerly – examples include the frequent changes in the structure of the NHS, the centralisation of direction about education, the visionary scheme for Universal Credit. The National Audit Office has been critical. They comment, for example, in respect of the major projects undertaken by the Department for Work and Pensions:

> The Department has had to deal with an unprecedented number of major programmes and reforms. … Any large portfolio of reforms will run into problems. The Department has shown a resolute approach to dealing with them. However, we think it has relied too much on dealing with difficulties as they emerge rather than anticipating what might go wrong. As a result it has had to learn some hard lessons with significant financial and human costs.[27]

On the integration of health and social care, similarly, they report: 'Integrating the health and social care sectors is a significant challenge in normal times, let alone times when both sectors are under such severe pressure. So far, benefits have fallen far short of plans, despite much effort.'[28]

---

[26] C A R Crosland, 1956, *The future of socialism*, London: Jonathan Cape, p 216.

[27] National Audit Office, 2015, *Welfare reform: lessons learned*, London: Department of Work and Pensions, https://www.nao.org.uk/report/welfare-reform-lessons-learned/, HC77, p 6.

[28] National Audit Office, 2017, Health and social care integration, HC1011 and NAO website, https://www.nao.org.uk/report/health-and-social-care-integration/

Bob Hudson has commented, trenchantly, that the latest White Paper on integration:

> takes a traditional view within central government that organisational restructuring can solve problems. This flies in the face of evidence that past attempts to do so have underestimated the associated costs and disruption. The 2012 Health and Social Care Act abolished strategic health authorities and primary care trusts, created clinical commissioning groups and NHS England, and cost an estimated £3 billion. Now, it's all change again despite having little to show for the previous exercise.[29]

The bulk of this book has been concerned with service delivery rather than institutional reform. Although I have suggested various ideas for reform, I have not developed any fully fleshed-out proposals. I have not, for example, tried to include costings, indicators or a strategy for implementation; they would only be relevant for a short period of time, and in a book of this kind I think it is more important to establish general principles.

If reforms are to be effective, they need to be practical. The ideas I have been putting forward have been guided by three considerations. First, I have sought to use and build on mechanisms that have been shown to work in other contexts. For example, the case that universal distribution can work is demonstrated by Child Benefit, Winter Fuel Payment and Google. Second, I have looked for ways to reduce the size of the problems. Most reforms will not necessarily solve problems, or prevent them, but they can help at least to whittle down the size of the problems which have to be dealt with. I have argued, among other things, that child protection could be helped by better child care; that the use of employment services could be reduced by a programme of public employment; that homelessness would be reduced by housebuilding. A third guiding principle can be found in the attempt to recognise that the situations which have to be dealt with are complex, and complexity has to be managed. I have argued for partial responses rather than comprehensive ones, defining clear divisions of labour, avoiding interactions between benefits and services, and more generally opting for policies which require less fine detail or fine-tuning by government agencies.

There are dangers in over-generalisation; there is no single, overarching solution to everything. I have pointed instead to a series of reforms, specific to the fields of activity they relate to. Table 11.1 briefly summarises the main points.

---

[29] B Hudson, 2021, *Short on detail but not on ambition: four problems with the new NHS White Paper*, https://www.transformingsociety.co.uk/2021/02/15/short-on-detail-but-not-on-ambition-four-problems-with-the-new-nhs-white-paper/

Table 11.1: Repairing the welfare state

Area	Issues	Distractions and false trails	Solutions
Social security	Safety nets and basic income Income packages	The obsession with work Selectivity	Smaller benefits More universality More predictability A universal basic pension
Health	Health care is not the same thing as health The dominance of university medicine	Marketisation Individualisation	Tiered decentralisation
Social care	The shift from health care Responding to personal needs	Personalisation; individualised budgeting	Developing a personal service: allocation of time rather than tasks
Education	The education system: primary, secondary and tertiary	Equal opportunity in an unequal society	Human development: a stronger focus on primary and elementary education
Child protection	Assumptions about the family The need for a residual service	Troubled families; inter-generational dependency	Child care Protection from physical assault
Housing	Shortages have consequences Structural disadvantage Access and deprivation	Tenure Affordability Individual pathology	Public housebuilding Urban regeneration
Employment	Structural unemployment	'Active' labour market policy Microeconomics Muddled with social security	Job creation Public employment
Equalities and human rights	Legal redress Discrimination and disadvantage	Human rights rather than the social rights of citizenship	Using legal protections; improving access to justice
Public services	Decommodification Services for everyone, and services for anyone	Market provision	Extending universality

After the pandemic: a new social settlement?

In the wake of the pandemic, it seems clear that many people would like to see a new social settlement. All the main political parties promise to rebuild, whatever that means; there is at least a renewed sense of our inter-dependency and the way our lives are bound up with other people's. Some accounts in the press of the social changes taking place are highly optimistic about what they can mean for society. We won't make the same mistakes again, the argument runs. We won't pare public provision down to the bone. We won't close down social protection. The response to the virus shows a sense of solidarity, of mutual responsibility, of common purpose.

In previous writing, I have emphasised the strength of solidaristic social networks. Everything we do is conditioned by our relationships with other people, and organisations and groups are fundamental to the way we live.[30] Given that position, I am not going to express surprise about the degree to which people have responded to the crisis by trying to help others in their community, or put themselves forward as public servants or volunteers – that is exactly what we should expect. It's basic to who we are, and what we are. At the same time, it is very uncertain whether the experience of the pandemic will lead to a new social settlement. The danger is that the opposite may be true. Social distancing and isolation imply a degree of dissociation from other people. It depends on atomisation – turning us into separate, distinctly individual units, centred on the household. That threatens our engagement with other people – how we do things, how we think about ourselves, and how we interact with others. It would be nice to think that the reaction to isolation will lead to everyone wanting to do the opposite when the restrictions are lifted, but there's little reason to suppose that will be the case. There are famous accounts of the atomisation of American society – David Riesman's book, *The lonely crowd*,[31] or Robert Putnam's *Bowling alone*.[32] That was the world we were heading towards before this crisis happened. The problem with social distancing is, bluntly, that people may have become used to it. If that has happened, it will accelerate the process of individualisation, putting us at a distance from everyone else. We should all be concerned.

Before the pandemic, the prescriptions of neoliberalism – the powerful emphasis on individual self-sufficiency, the idea that markets and business do things better, or that welfare needs to be more personal and choice-based – had come to dominate arguments about welfare. There are alternatives to the neoliberal approach; I would point in particular to two discrete, but

---

[30] P Spicker, 2019, *Thinking collectively*, Bristol: Policy Press.

[31] D Riesman, 1961, *The lonely crowd*, New Haven: Yale University Press.

[32] R Putnam, 2001, *Bowling alone*, New York: Simon & Schuster.

complementary, counter-narratives. One is individualistic, but it is from a different school of individualism than the negativity of the radical right. Individualism can offer people a sense of dignity, mutual respect and worth, and human rights. This kind of individualism was powerfully influential in the development of social services, and it can be taken to justify a wide range of activities in what is now thought of as a 'welfare state'. Table 11.2 is drawn from the conclusion of my book, *Reclaiming individualism*.[33]

Table 11.2: Social policy on individualist principles

	Rights	Basic security	Empowerment
Universal standards	Citizenship	Minimum income standards	Voting
Common interests	Community safety – for example, fire services, coastguard	Medical care	Access to information
Shared objectives	Housing standards and provision; minimum income standards	Securing economic prosperity; public health	Education
Protecting individuals	Social care	Child protection; employment protection	Redress

The other main narrative is social. The welfare state is a collective ideal, based in a sense of mutual responsibility and solidarity. The idea of a common good can be interpreted in several ways – as the sum of individual goods, as common ground, and as social well-being; it is also, for many of its advocates, about collective action and joint enterprise. The principles that informed the foundation of the welfare state are still sound. The programmes have, for the most part, huge popular support. The welfare state has had a profound effect on well-being, security and disadvantage. The provision of welfare protects people's rights, both human rights and their rights as citizens. It has played a major part in securing for ordinary people the conditions of civilisation. It is a major expression of the obligations we have to each other. And the process of collective action makes us a more decent society: a better place to live.

---

[33] Spicker, 2013, p 200.

Afterword: a personal note

Most of my career has been concerned with social policy and administration, whether that was done through study, practice, teaching or writing. I began with housing, serving as a voluntary advisor when I was a student and then taking a job as lettings officer in a local authority housing department. My interest in social security came about because it was such a large part of work in housing rights; I became a voluntary representative while studying law, and later I moved on to teach, write and research in the area. Teaching social workers led me to work on health and social care, including research on mental health and dementia. As a carer, I have encountered more recently many of the same problems in mental health services that I first became aware of as a researcher. And then, as a jobbing policy analyst, I would be asked to find out about a range of topics from the point of view of service professionals and users, including work on poverty, homelessness and disability. Much of this book has been built on a flow of insights, experiences and conversations with practitioners and service users. Those exchanges have fed into and reinforced a generally critical (and occasionally jaded) view of how social services work.

This will not be my last book, but it might have been. In May 2020, a few weeks into lockdown, I was diagnosed with a variant of blood cancer that would, only a few years before, have been considered terminal. Despite the crisis that was gripping the NHS, I received urgent attention from the GP, rapid admission to hospital (less than two hours after blood tests), the work of a suite of specialist consultants, a dedicated nursing team, and the laboratories in England and Scotland who analysed the condition. I was lucky in other ways. The illness was rare but appeared to be treatable, by a drug initially approved for another purpose. There were not enough case examples to justify a formal validation of the treatment, but the lead consultant asked the Scottish Medicines Consortium for permission to prescribe it, and the approval came through within twenty minutes. The performance of the NHS was, then, outstanding, and my appraisal of the service is possibly coloured by the fact that it has just saved my life.

I have had to make certain adjustments to my way of working; I am somewhat less mobile than I was. My new physical limitations have made it difficult for me to carry on with the kind peripatetic engagement with the field that I have been doing for much of my career. But I could still write, and there were things I wanted to write about. As a teacher, I have spent much of my career offering balanced arguments; as a researcher, my main task has been to listen to other people. It was past time that I should express some views of my own.

This is, then, a personal account of the welfare state. I know, of course, that there are many sides to the arguments, and that reasonable people might reasonably hold different views; I do not have all the answers. I hope the positions I take will prompt people to think more directly about the way that things are done, and to ask whether they could not be done better. My object, however, has been to get readers to think critically about social services; if you have agreed with every word in this book, I will be disappointed.

Paul Spicker

Index